PELICAN BOOKS

A 577

THE DANCER'S HERITAGE

IVOR GUEST

IVOR GUEST

The Dancer's Heritage

A SHORT HISTORY OF BALLET

WITH A FOREWORD BY
DAME MARGOT FONTEYN, D.B.E.
AND TWENTY-FOUR PLATES

PENGUIN BOOKS
BALTIMORE · MARYLAND

Penguin Books Ltd, Harmondsworth, Middlesex
U.S.A.: Penguin Books Inc., 3300 Clipper Mill Road, Baltimore 11, Md
AUSTRALIA: Penguin Books Pty Ltd, 762 Whitehorse Road,
Mitcham, Victoria

—

First published by A. and C. Black 1960
This revised edition published in Pelican Books 1962

—

—

Made and printed in Great Britain
by Cox and Wyman Ltd,
London, Reading, and Fakenham
Set in Monotype Garamond

This book is dedicated to
DAME ADELINE GENÉE, D.B.E.

Contents

Foreword

BY DAME MARGOT FONTEYN, D.B.E.

MR GUEST has given us a wonderful book full of interesting historical details. There is much here for young dancers to learn, particularly in relation to style, which is the most important single aspect of ballet in need of attention, now that the technical standard is so generally high and there is such a wealth of good ballets to be danced.

The contemporary ballets are the least problem of course, because the living choreographer conveys his personal conception of the ballet vocabulary while creating his works. But even then they are difficult to preserve intact for long periods without very careful supervision. Little touches get lost here and there with each change of cast, and only the choreographer himself can really re-inspire the production.

As for the great ballets of the past, there is often no one at all to guide us on the sometimes tiny details of movement, without which we cannot re-create its true atmosphere.

It seems increasingly important for dancers to develop in themselves a greater awareness of the different choreographic styles they may encounter in a normal ballet repertoire.

In the case of the old traditional ballets which have been handed down from generation to generation, often unrecorded, particular thought and attention should be given to the conditions surrounding their original creation. No one can be sure of the exact steps, but one can form some idea of their presentation by considering the social and artistic life of the time and the prevailing system of training. To this end we should study the general history of ballet as well as the lives of those immortals who have contributed to its evolution as an art throughout the centuries.

Each period demands a subtly different style.

9

The accent on gracious charm in the Romantic ballets reflected the manners of the time, just as Fokine's far greater freedom of expression was born of an age that also produced Isadora Duncan. Our own day seems to bring forth many ballets of violence and blue jeans tempered by the exacting, glacial, abstract ballet – these at least are the important new trends among many excellent but less adventurous works.

We should be inherently aware of this historical aspect of our art, and project each role within the framework of its time, otherwise all ballets become a meaningless series of steps arranged in various combinations. On the dramatic plane too the same rules apply. Giselle's mad scene for instance, although it has to be completely convincing, must remain within the bounds of nineteenth-century romanticism. It would lose its pathos if performed with the distressing realism of some of the more contemporary ballets.

The public today show an unprecedented interest in ballet which only the highest artistic levels will be able to maintain for long. It is therefore a key moment, now, for dancers to assimilate their great heritage from the past whilst developing the extraordinary opportunities of the present, so that they can pass easily from one to the other displaying the full richness of this wonderful art. Only then will we be worthy of the immortals who are so faithfully re-created for us in this book.

To the Reader

THE purpose of this book is a modest one. It is to provide an introduction to the history of ballet and to give an idea of how the art which flourishes today on the stages of Covent Garden and other theatres throughout the world has been built up over the centuries. The work of countless choreographers, dancers, teachers, musicians, and others of the past has lived on to form the tradition that is every dancer's heritage. This tradition is the backbone of ballet. Dance technique, for instance, has become what it is today through having been passed on from generation to generation, becoming all the time more and more elaborate and complex. And in the same way the repertory of ballets that are performed is continually being enriched by works which will become classics in their turn; today we can see ballets that were first performed by the Paris Opéra Ballet and the Royal Danish Ballet of the Romantic period a hundred years and more ago, by the Imperial Russian Ballet, and by the Diaghilev Ballet, and no doubt several ballets that have been created in recent years will continue to be danced for the pleasure of future generations.

This tradition is not a dead thing, for what is being done today will become the history of tomorrow. History should not, therefore, be looked upon as a useless subject. It is, in fact, of great value both for the dancer and for the spectator. The dancer it can help to understand the styles of the various ballets in the repertory, while for the spectator it will sharpen his critical faculty and give him a background of knowledge against which he can appreciate what he sees. History need not be dull and dry-as-dust, for it is mainly about men and women who lived, worked, and loved in days gone by, who had much the same feelings and reactions, qualities and failings, as those who make up the ballet world today. Approached in this way, it can come alive and acquire a special significance.

The aim of this book is no more than to introduce the reader to some of the people who have helped to make ballet history and to tell a little of their triumphs, their struggles, and their ideas. In the hope that it will whet the reader's appetite and tempt him to delve further into the subject, I have added at the end a selected list of more specialized books in English which are either in print or should be obtainable from a public library. For those who want to inquire still more deeply, some of these books contain more exhaustive bibliographies in cluding works by foreign writers. For there is really no end to this sort of research; to the imaginative reader the study of history can be as exciting and rewarding as a voyage of discovery.

CHAPTER ONE

When Kings and Princes Danced

To trace the origins of dancing, if that were possible, we should have to go back, certainly, far beyond the beginnings of history and into the mists of prehistoric times. Probably we should arrive at the moment when a living creature developed the first glimmering of what was to become the mind and soul of man, and even then our quest might not be ended. The art of the theatre which we call ballet, however, is of much later origin. It is in fact an art of recent times, and emerges some five hundred years ago during the period known as the Renaissance – the very starting-point of modern history.

The word renaissance, which means rebirth, aptly describes the development in man's outlook that was gathering force in Italy when England was struggling through the Wars of the Roses. During the Middle Ages individuality had counted for very little, but in the fourteenth and fifteenth centuries new lines of thought – which we call humanism – were beginning to be explored that were concerned more with the affairs of man than with the abstract conceptions which had obsessed the older school of thinkers. As a result the most astonishing progress was made, not only in philosophy but in the sciences and the arts and indeed in every branch of human endeavour.

Italy, where this development first bore fruit, was in those days a patchwork of states, some large, some small, whose rulers were as cunning in intrigue and diplomacy as they were adept in furthering their own personal prestige. It mattered greatly to these rulers that they should appear important and imposing in the eyes of their neighbours, and so they made every effort to give brilliance to their courts, particularly when there was question of a marriage that involved an alliance with another ruling house. In this way the more enlightened of these princes became patrons of a flourishing culture and provided artists, philosophers, and scientists with the conditions and opportunities which made possible the fabulous achievements of the High Renaissance.

This was the setting for the appearance of the earliest professional dancing-masters, who were often important figures at these Italian courts. Under their influence, dancing developed from a pastime into an art possessing a definite technique which they evolved, elaborated, and codified, and from which our present ballet technique has sprung.

The first of these masters whose name is known to us was Domenico of Piacenza. His pupils called him the 'King of the Art', and for many years he was in the service of the Estes, the ruling family of Ferrara. Shortly after 1400, he wrote a treatise on dancing which is the earliest known work of its kind, but the dance technique which he describes in it was almost certainly not invented by him but handed down to him by earlier masters whose names have not survived. Written before the invention of printing, this precious manuscript is more than a manual of technique, for we learn from it the very important fact that Domenico created dances. About twenty of these dances are actually described.

Other dances created by Domenico were recorded by his followers Antonio Cornazano and William the Jew, who about half a century later also wrote treatises, which show how much richer the technique had then become. Cornazano was a poet as well as a dancing-master who worked for the Sforzas in Milan and for the Estes, while William the Jew was in such demand that he travelled widely all over Italy, producing dances for important state occasions here, there, and everywhere. Not only did he become a favourite both of Lorenzo the Magnificent, the Medici ruler of Florence, and of the cruel art-loving Galeazzo Sforza, Duke of Milan, to whom he dedicated his book, but he was also knighted in Venice by the Holy Roman Emperor.

Many of the dances produced by these early masters expressed some interplay of feelings between the performers, such as the rivalry of a group of young men for a girl's favours or the spurning of an unwelcome suitor's attentions. These *balli* or *balletti*, as they were called, so caught the fancy of the time that before long the dance began to penetrate nearly every form of spectacle to be seen in Italy. It had always been an important feature of the festivities which the princes of the Renaissance commanded to mark special occasions, but soon even the sacred mysteries of Florence were being given with interludes of dancing, and during the sixteenth century the dance was to find a place in the developing arts of drama, pastorale, and opera.

When King Charles VIII of France crossed the Alps with his army in 1494 to claim the throne of Naples, he and his courtiers were astonished at the wealth of dancing they found. The magnificence of the court entertainments in Milan, Ferrara, and elsewhere must have dazzled them almost into disbelief. For often no expense would be spared, and the greatest artists of the time would contribute their services. The father of Raphael had organized one of these performances at Urbino in 1488, in which about a hundred dancers took part, and for another, which was staged at Milan in 1496, the costumes of the dancers and some marvellous effects were designed by Leonardo da Vinci.

Sometimes these entertainments, even though they were produced for only a single occasion, achieved a renown that extended far beyond the borders of the state where they originated. One example was Bergonzio di Botta's 'dinner-ballet' which was staged at Tortona in 1489 to celebrate the marriage of the Duke of Milan. A modern spectator might be reminded of an elaborate floor-show, for it was given to entertain the guests during the banquet and each scene had a theme taken from classical legend and suggested by the course of the meal it accompanied. There were many spectacular surprises and many delicate allusions to the bridal couple, and a large part of the entertainment was given over to dancing. A mimic hunt preceded the course of wild boar, and the fish was introduced with a magnificent ballet of the gods of the sea and earth and rivers of Lombardy. As the banquet drew to a close, the guests were treated to an allegorical ballet extolling the virtues of happy married life, and the evening's entertainment gaily closed with the arrival of Bacchus and Silenus.

The French discovery of Italian culture was to have far-reaching consequences in the development of ballet. For a long time dancing had been a courtly recreation in France, where there had been entertainments called 'mascarades' which bore a certain primitive resemblance to the ballets of later times, and in which the King himself had sometimes taken part. One of these, the *Bal des Ardens* of 1393, was long remembered because of its macabre climax, when the weak-minded Charles VI so nearly lost his life. He and five of his gentlemen entered the ballroom dressed up as savages in tight-fitting costumes covered all over with tow and connected to each other with a chain. None of the spectators was sure of their identity, and as they were dancing, the King's ambitious brother, the Duke of Orleans, peered closely to see through their disguise and set fire to the inflammable costumes with his torch. By a stroke of fortune, just before this happened, the King had released himself from the chain and gone to speak to the Duchess of Berry, who protected him by throwing the train of her dress over him. Of his five companions, only one, who managed to break the chain and threw himself into a tub of water, survived. These mascarades, however, followed no set form and were often little more than a means of revelry. It was only with the appearance of Italian dancing-masters at the French court that dancing became a refined and essential courtly accomplishment and the seeds of the French court ballet were sown.

One of the first Italian dancing-masters to enter the service of the King of France was Pompeo Diobono, who was brought to Paris from Milan by Marshal de Brissac. At the same time, the Marshal dispatched a band of Italian musicians, among whom was a performer of such extraordinary talent that he was to be acknowledged as 'the finest violinist in Christendom' – Baltazarini di Belgiojoso. Beaujoyeulx, as he became known in France, was appointed a court valet to

Catherine de' Medici, who virtually ruled the kingdom during the reigns of her sons, Charles IX and Henri III. Catherine was a firm believer in magnificence and before long Beaujoyeulx found himself entrusted with the task of producing court festivities on the Italian scale. For this he was well equipped. He was steeped in the Milanese tradition of court entertainments, and since his arrival in France he had absorbed other influences. The theories of the short-lived Académie de Musique et de Poésie, which aimed at combining music and verse and movement, made a deep impression on him, and so did the Italian tragedies and pastorales with danced interludes which he saw performed by Italian players in Paris. These were the principal factors that decided the form of his most famous work, the *Balet Comique de la Royne*.

This was produced in 1581 as part of the festivities for the marriage of Marguerite of Lorraine, the sister of Henri III's queen, Louise. The performance took place in the Grand Hall of the Petit-Bourbon Palace, which was next to the Louvre, and we have a good idea of what this ballet looked like, because an illustrated description was afterwards printed and distributed abroad for propaganda purposes. There was no stage as we know it, the action taking place on the floor of the hall, with the crowded audience accommodated in two galleries extending round three of the walls, the King, Catherine de' Medici, and the more distinguished spectators being seated on a dais at one end. Opposite them scenery represented the Palace of Circe, and in the middle of the hall were various properties such as a grove of trees and a golden vault covered with clouds. The ballet was a mixture of music and song, declamation, dance and spectacle, which Beaujoyeulx claimed was a new form and to which he gave the name 'ballet-comique' to convey that the dance and the drama (*comédie* in French) were combined to make a unified whole. It lasted for some six hours and, with much elaboration, told how the enchantress Circe overcame Apollo and the Gods but had to bow before the majesty of the King of France. One of the most splendid moments was the entrance of Queen Louise and some of her ladies, in a golden car that spouted water like a glorious fountain, with sirens and tritons, singing and playing musical instruments, in attendance. Finally the entertainment ended at about three o'clock in the morning with the grand ballet.

Because he had to arrange the dances to be seen from above and from three sides, Beaujoyeulx was faced with very different problems from those of today's choreographers whose ballets are designed to be seen only from the front. The patterns on the floor which the dancers made as they moved were therefore more important than their individual technique, and in the days of the court ballet, geometry was considered to be an essential part of a choreographer's knowledge.

The fame of the *Balet Comique de la Royne* and later French court ballets tended to overshadow important activities elsewhere. In England the court entertainment took the form of the masque, which began to emerge when Henry VIII was a young man and reached its peak in the reign of James I. The elaborate masques which were produced at Whitehall, with their fanciful scenarios by Ben Jonson and their spectacular scenery and effects by Inigo Jones, an artist in the Italian tradition, were the courtly counterparts of the great tragedies and comedies by Shakespeare which were drawing the public to the Globe Theatre on the other side of the River Thames. The masque, being more of a literary spectacle than a ballet, was a typically English form of entertainment, and when other European countries, such as Denmark, adopted the court ballet, it was to France and the splendour of the court at Versailles that they turned for an example.

While French predominance was slowly but surely making itself felt in the evolution of ballet, important activities were still taking place in Italy. In Turin, early in the seventeenth century, the prolific Count Filippo d'Agliè produced a series of brilliant ballets. Italy also led in matters of technique, as the writings of Caroso and Negri show us. Caroso's *Il Ballerino* came out in 1581, the same year as the *Balet Comique de la Royne*, and Negri's *The Graces of Love* is dated 1604. These two technical manuals show the progress which had been made since the days of William the Jew. Virtuosity was still the preserve of the male dancer, by whom beaten steps and turns were much practised, and Negri's book contains the earliest known reference to a *plié*, which was advised for giving added effect to jumps and such steps as *capriolles*. But as yet the legs were not turned out from the thigh: that was to be developed gradually during the seventeenth and eighteenth centuries.

The court ballet maintained its popularity in France for nearly a hundred years. The death of Catherine de' Medici made little difference, for dancing had become accepted as a necessary grace and Henri IV, Louis XIII, and Louis XIV all stimulated the development of ballet by the personal interest they took in it. Under Henri IV, the ballet-comique with its continuous plot, which was usually inspired by mythology, gave place to the simpler ballet-mascarade consisting mainly of burlesque scenes, or *entrées* as they were called, with generally little, if any, plot to connect them. Far from being pompous and tedious, these ballet-mascarades were vital and amusing. They were full of allusions to happenings and personalities of the time, introduced comic characters such as laundrywomen and innkeepers, and were enlivened by droll and grotesque effects. Henri IV delighted in watching these entertainments, and fell in love for the last time in his life when he saw the lovely Charlotte de Montmorency at a rehearsal of one of them. As for his queen, Marie de' Medici, she so lived up to the family tradition that it was said she could not do without her ballets even when she was in mourning. The courtiers naturally followed the royal example, and the passion for ballet became so widespread that even the nation's greatest soldiers were infected with it. The Marshal de Bassompierre could not get it out of his system, and once, as he was about to storm a fortress, he turned to his staff with the words: 'The décor and the dancers are ready – now the ballet can begin.'

During the succeeding reign of Louis XIII, sung recitative replaced declamation, and the court ballet entered a new phase. In the early years of the reign, when the Duke of Luynes was

Intendant of the Court Pleasures, a form of melodramatic ballet emerged, in which music played a more important part and the subject was often based on a heroic or romantic theme. One such ballet was *La Délivrance de Renaud*, which told the story of Rinaldo and Armida and was produced in 1617 with the ulterior motive of reassuring the ambassadors of Austria and Spain that all was well with the King's marriage.

When the Duke of Nemours took over the duties of Luynes in 1621, another type of ballet developed – the *ballet à entrée*, which consisted of a number of independent sketches, often of a grotesque or vulgar character, linked only by some general idea. One of the most successful of these burlesque ballets was the *Grand Ballet de la Douairière de Billebahaut*, given in 1626. The form of the *ballet à éntrée* was continued in a more serious manner after the death of Nemours, when Cardinal Richelieu organized a series of ballets to celebrate such events as the birth of the Dauphin, the future Louis XIV, and France's military triumphs in the Thirty Years War.

Louis XIII, who had a special gift for comedy, danced in many court ballets, and on one occasion he devised a whole ballet himself. It was in his reign, from about 1630, that the general public was first allowed to watch some of these ballets. By then professional dancers had already begun to appear, at first playing mostly comic and character roles, and never taking part in the grand ballet at the end, which was reserved for the King and his courtiers.

The court ballet entered its final and most brilliant phase under Louis XIV. During the early years of his reign, when his mother, Anne of Austria, ruled as regent, the introduction of Italian opera into France caused a momentary decline in the production of court ballets. But from the day in 1651 when the twelve-year-old King danced in his first ballet, *Cassandre*, the court ballet once more came into its own. Louis XIV took his kingship very seriously, and his sense of divine mission may well have been stimulated by his playing such roles as the Rising Sun and Apollo during the impressionable years of his adolescence and early manhood. The ballets of his reign were much more refined than those of his father's time, and most of them took the form of *ballets à entrée*, such as the *Ballet de l'Impatience*, which illustrated various aspects of impatience.

Realizing that art could be made to enhance his prestige as a monarch, the King chose men of real talent to produce the ballets which added so much to the brilliance of his court. The librettos were mostly written by an established playwright, Isaac de Benserade, whose elegant verses were matched by the music of Jean-Baptiste Lully. Lully, who had come to France from Florence as a boy, first attracted notice at court as a comic dancer who could make the King laugh until the tears streamed down his cheeks. Being also a very talented violinist, he became a member of the King's band and, before he was twenty, he was appointed Composer of Instrumental Music. His music for the court ballets reflected his lively character and must have provided added inspiration for the choreographer, who invariably was a professional dancer. The most famous choreographer of this period was Charles-Louis Beauchamps, who also invented a system of notation for recording dances and was a fine teacher, like his uncle Pierre who had taught the King. The five positions of the feet were then just beginning to be accepted as the basis of technique, and Beauchamps is supposed to have been the first to define them.

Having been well trained as a dancer, Louis XIV appreciated the value of good teaching, and in 1661 he founded the Académie Royale de Danse. This consisted of thirteen dancing-masters, who were given the task of 're-establishing the art in its perfection'. A room in the Louvre was set aside for their meetings, but they preferred to gather in the freer atmosphere of a nearby tavern called L'Epée de Bois. The importance of this Académie lay not in what it achieved – for it was never incorporated in the Paris Opéra and it finally petered out towards the end of the eighteenth century – but in the mere fact that it was established. For it was the first time that royal recognition had been given to dance teaching.

The dance had not yet become wholly separated from song and the spoken word, so that Molière's conception of the comédie-ballet was quite a logical development. Molière, one of the greatest of French playwrights, had been educated at one of the Jesuit colleges where it was customary to produce classical plays with danced interludes, and in later years, when he was the leader of a troupe of actors, he thought of the idea of introducing dancing into his plays. His first comédie-ballet was *Les Fâcheux*, which he wrote for a magnificent fête with which Fouquet, the minister of finance, was planning to entertain Louis XIV. Its form was apparently accidental. He had been asked to arrange a ballet as well as write a comedy. But there were so few good dancers available that he decided to insert the *entrées* of the ballet between the scenes of the play to allow the dancers time to change their costumes. Further, so as not to interrupt the comedy's plot too much, the danced interludes were closely linked to the text with the result that comedy and ballet combined to form a work that was complete in itself. The King's delight at the piece did not save Fouquet from disgrace, but it confirmed Molière in the royal favour which he was to enjoy for the remaining years of his life.

Molière repeated this successful formula several times afterwards, with Lully composing the music and Beauchamps arranging the dances. In 1670 this wonderful combination produced the most famous of all comédie-ballets, *Le Bourgeois Gentilhomme*, in which Lully had the role of his life as the Mufti. Molière was by then a sick man, and was to die only three years later, within a few hours of acting the leading part in his last comédie-ballet, *Le Malade imaginaire*. During his last years he had to struggle for the right to produce his works in their original form, for his former collaborator Lully, who had then become one of the directors of the newly-founded Opéra, contended that he had the sole privilege to produce ballet. After Molière's death, the dance element in his works was looked upon as of little importance, and in a very short time dwindled away completely.

By this time the court ballet was fast declining. The King had ceased to dance in 1670. It was said that he had taken to heart some verses in Racine's tragedy *Britannicus* about Nero's passion for performing before his subjects, but he was also growing stout, although only in his early thirties. Louis XIV's retirement as an active dancer removed the incentive for his courtiers to dance, but the days of the court ballet were inevitably numbered, for the age of absolutism, of which the court ballet was an expression, was approaching its decline. It was only the professional dancers who now had a real interest in keeping the art of ballet alive in France, and being no longer able to exercise their talents fully at court, they turned to the theatre for employment.

CHAPTER TWO

Ballet Enters the Theatre

SHORTLY before he sounded the death-knell of the court
ballet by ceasing to dance himself, Louis XIV ensured the
continuing existence of ballet in France by granting a privilege
for an opera house to be founded in Paris. The Paris Opéra
that we know today traces its history back to this privilege,
granted in 1669. Since then it has seen many homes, the first
of which was a converted tennis-court not far from Saint-
Germain-des-Prés.

This makeshift theatre opened in 1671 with an opera called
Pomone, which included dances arranged by Beauchamps and
ran for eight months. The new venture then collapsed, not
because it proved unpopular, but because the management and
the financiers fell out among themselves. Lully, who had at
first been sceptical about the future of opera, then saw his
opportunity. By devious means he managed to have the
privilege transferred to himself, and moved the Opéra, first
to a rickety tennis-court nearby, and shortly afterwards to
safer quarters in the Palais Royal. Taking over the theatre
in the Palais Royal meant turning out the troupe of actors
which his former colleague Molière had founded, but Lully's
ambition overrode the scruples of his conscience, if he had
any.

Until his death in 1687 Lully remained so all-powerful at the
head of the Paris Opéra that every work produced there during
that time was composed by himself. *Divertissements* formed an
important part of his operas, these being usually arranged by
Beauchamps. But Lully's collaboration with Molière had
taught him how the dance could be woven into an opera so as
to fit in with the action, and his own training as a dancer enabled him to take an active hand in the choreography when-

ever he wanted to achieve a particular effect or arrange some comic passage.

In the Opéra's early days, there were not enough professional dancers available, and several noblemen had become so proficient and keen that Louis XIV gave them special permission to appear on the stage without losing their rank. At first only male dancers were seen, women's roles being taken by men in travesty and wearing masks. But it was not long before women, wearing heavy long dresses reaching almost to the ground, took their place alongside the men who wore masks and costumes after the military fashion of the ancient Romans for 'noble' dancing, or fantastic clothes incorporating realistic symbols – such as shoes for a shoemaker, musical instruments for music, and so on – for character parts. In 1681 four ballerinas took the stage in Lully's opera *Le Triomphe de l'Amour*. Their leader, Mlle Lafontaine, thus became the Opéra's first prima ballerina. However, for some time they continued to be very much overshadowed by the men, and although Mlle Lafontaine danced at the Opéra for ten years or more and was known as 'the Queen of the Dance', we know nothing of her style. Indeed, the only detail we know about that of her successor, Marie-Thérèse de Subligny is the bare fact that her legs were not well turned out – a reminder that women's technique in France was still in a rudimentary stage.

As the Opéra's company of dancers became increasingly proficient and numerous, the dance itself became more and more popular with the Paris public and a new type of opera began to appear. This was the opera-ballet, which comprised a number of *divertissements* or *entrées* linked together by some common idea in the theme. As the name opera-ballet implies, the dancing and singing were of equal importance. Indeed, many people were drawn to the Opéra by the attraction of the ballet, and the composer Campra, whose *L'Europe Galante* was one of the earliest examples of this sort of work, saw to the heart of the matter when he remarked that the only way of making opera-ballet really popular was to lengthen the dances and shorten the ballerinas' skirts.

The opera-ballet retained its vogue until well into the eighteenth century, reaching its highest level, artistically and musically, in the works of Jean-Philippe Rameau, who was a contemporary of Handel. Rameau's finest opera-ballet was *Les Indes Galantes*, which was first produced in 1735 and was spectacularly revived at the Opéra as recently as 1952. These opera-ballets were rather like programmes of one-act *divertissements*, each introduced by a short operatic scene. The balance of such a work was seldom disturbed by the addition of another *entrée*, as happened with *Les Indes Galantes*, and for many years the Opéra used to give programmes called *Fragments*, which consisted of *entrées* taken from different opera-ballets.

What the recent revival of *Les Indes Galantes* brought out so clearly was the splendour of the production, which was a feature of the opera-ballets of the eighteenth century – and indeed of the operas of Lully before them, most of which were designed by Jean Bérain. Noverre, who could remember the opera-house in the Palais Royal where all the great French opera-ballets were produced, was struck by the contrast between the dirty, badly-lit auditorium, from many parts of which it was impossible to obtain an adequate view of the stage, and the magnificence of the scenery and the precision and efficiency of the stage machinery. Servandoni, one of the greatest scene designers of his time, designed some brilliant scenery for the flower *divertissement* in *Les Indes Galantes*, and reproduced the eruption of a volcano for another scene in the same production.

It had soon become necessary to ensure a continuous supply of proficient dancers, and in 1713 the School of Dance was established at the Paris Opéra. We know about the technique that was taught there at that time from Feuillet's book *Chorégraphie*, first published in 1700, which describes a system for notating dances. There was still much in common between theatrical and social dancing, although the technique of the former was more elaborate. The hall-marks of the French school were grace, charm, and elegance. Virtuosity was not sought after as an end in itself, and steps of elevation, such as were much practised in Italy, were only sparingly used. Already the technical vocabulary of a dancer included many steps with which we are familiar today, such as *entrechats*, *sissonnes*, *cabrioles*, *coupés*, and *chassés*.

Many of these steps – the *entrechat*, for instance – were at first performed only by male dancers. For in the beginning it was the male dancers who were the great personalities of French ballet. The great Beauchamps himself, the Opéra's first ballet-master, was a vigorous dancer who was unsurpassed for his turning. When Lully died, he retired from the theatre and was succeeded by Louis Pécour, many of whose dances are recorded for us in Feuillet's notation – *pas de deux* for the most part, set down as they were danced by Subligny, Balon, Blondy, and other great dancers of the day. Jean Balon, in spite of his heeled shoes, which everyone wore then, danced with such prodigious lightness that it became widely but probably erroneously supposed that the term *ballon*, which expresses the springiness of a dancer's jump, was derived from his name. He was a great favourite with Louis XIV and had the rare privilege of being permitted to shake the King by the hand. Blondy was Beauchamp's nephew, and although he was to succeed Pécour as ballet-master of the Opéra, he was to be remembered mainly as a dancer – the greatest in Europe in his own sphere, it was said.

But these reputations paled before that of Louis Dupré, who was known as 'le grand Dupré' because of his commanding height and presence. He was specially noted for the harmony of his movements, particularly in *adage*, and he was known to his contemporaries as 'the God of the Dance'. He danced at the Opéra until he was about sixty, becoming ever statelier as the years went by. Casanova saw this great dancer towards the end of his long career. He had been taken to the Opéra by a friend, and from his standing place – for there were no seats in the pit in those days – he saw a tall, elegant figure, wearing a mask and an enormous black wig reaching half way down his back, advance with measured steps to the front of the stage. 'The inimitable Dupré,' Casanova's friend explained amid the thunderous applause. The dance seemed to last not half a minute before this imposing creature vanished like a summer breeze into the wings to loud cries of 'Bravo!' Later on he returned to perform another dance, which seemed to Casanova to differ little from the first except at the end, when he moved towards the footlights and adopted a very fine pose. Suddenly excited exclamations broke out from all sides, and even Casanova stood entranced as Dupré's body seemed to stretch and stretch as though made of elastic.

Personalities, both male and female, were now emerging to catch the imagination of the public. Artists began to see dancers as ideal models, and one of the earliest and loveliest portraits of a ballerina is Raoux's painting of Françoise Prévost as a bacchante – an idealized portrait, however, for she would never have appeared so lightly clad on the stage. Ballerinas were still encumbered by long and heavy skirts that so prevented them from rivalling the male dancers in technique, that it could hardly have mattered very much that Mlles Subligny and Prévost were not well turned out, as their contemporaries observed. But this state of affairs did not last long, and with the appearance of the famous rival ballerinas, Camargo and Sallé, the supremacy of the male dancer was seriously challenged for the first time.

Although they were both pupils of Françoise Prévost, the styles of these two dancers, like their family backgrounds and their temperaments, could not have been more different. While rivalling one another for the public's enthusiasm, each in her own way set off the particular gifts of the other. For if Camargo in her prime was supreme as a virtuoso, Sallé had no equal as an expressive dancer. This contrast of styles was to be repeated in later periods, as we shall see by that of Taglioni and Elssler in the nineteenth century, and that of Ulanova and Lepeshinskaya in our own time.

First to appear at the Paris Opéra was the Brussels-born Marie-Anne de Cupis de Camargo, who took her name from her grandmother, a noblewoman of Spanish blood. Her début in 1726 was so successful that Françoise Prévost began to fear for her own position and saw that the new dancer was relegated to the ranks of the *corps de ballet*. Happily this petty scheming proved of no avail. One evening one of the male dancers missed his entrance, and seizing her opportunity, Camargo leapt forward and danced his *variation*. Her triumph was complete, and it was not long before Françoise Prévost bowed to the inevitable and retired.

Voltaire said that Camargo was the first ballerina to dance like a man. Brilliance of execution was the key to her style, which was perfected by three great male teachers – Pécour, Blondy, and Dupré – after Françoise Prévost had peevishly refused to give her any more classes. Before long Camargo was performing beaten steps such as *entrechats quatre*, which no woman had performed in Paris before, and for which she shortened her skirt by several inches to give her greater freedom of movement and allow these steps to be better seen. This was the first of many costume reforms that have come about through the increasing technical demands of choreographers.

Marie Sallé was a gentle creature and a model of virtue: another point of contrast with Camargo, who was the toast of Paris and notorious for her love affairs. Sallé's parents were simple players belonging to a small touring company which spent part of each year appearing at the popular theatres in the Fairs of Paris. Beginning her career as a child prodigy, she was delighting London audiences when she was nine at John Rich's theatre in Lincoln's Inn Fields. Legend has it that five years later she replaced Françoise Prévost at the Opéra one evening when that ballerina fell suddenly ill, but she did not make her official début there until 1727, a year after Camargo.

Marie Sallé commanded as many admirers in Paris as Camargo. Lancret was to paint portraits of both of them, and Voltaire wrote a poem tactfully extolling their respective talents without favouring either at the expense of the other. But while Camargo found ample scope for her sparkling little dances, Sallé soon found she could not express herself as she wished at the Paris Opéra. Twice she left in frustration. On the second occasion she only escaped being imprisoned – the penalty inflicted on refractory dancers – by crossing the

Channel. In London she found not only a warm welcome but the opportunities she desired. After producing and dancing in her most famous ballet, *Pigmalion*, at Covent Garden, she arranged several *divertissements* for Handel's operas. In time her differences with the Opéra were forgotten, and when she returned to Paris in 1735 she was re-engaged on better terms than ever and made her reappearance in the first performance of *Les Indes Galantes*. She danced as the Rose in the magical Ballet of Flowers – 'the most brilliant spectacle ever seen on the lyric stage', it was written – which she probably arranged herself. Her position at the Opéra seemed doubly secure now, for Camargo had temporarily retired from the stage. But soon there appeared an even more formidable rival.

This was a young Italian ballerina called Barberina, who was gifted not only with youth and beauty but with all the astonishing prowess of the Italian school of technique. In Italy, where the first public theatres had been established many years before those of Paris, the dance had long been the domain of professionals who not only had to entertain courtiers – for court ballets were still given when occasion required – but to hold the attention of a less refined public. Consequently the strong technique that had always been a feature of Italian dancing was developed to the point of virtuosity. Speed and brilliance, particularly in turns and jumps, were the hall-marks of the Italian technique that Barberina brought with her to Paris in 1739. The exploits of Camargo paled before the brilliance of Barberina, the French dancer's famous *entrechat quatre* appearing simple by comparison with the *entrechat huit* which the Italian seemed to perform with such nonchalant ease. This was a revelation to Paris, and a shock to Marie Sallé, whose retirement from the stage very shortly afterwards, when she was only thirty-two and still at the height of her powers, seemed an admission of defeat. She need have had no fears, however, for her position in the history of ballet was secure. This did not rest upon any exploits of technique, but in her efforts to reform the ballet by giving it more expression.

CHAPTER THREE

The Rise of the Choreographer

EXPRESSION and dance technique are the two main elements in choreography, and at any given moment in the history of ballet we shall nearly always find that one is in greater favour than the other. During one period, for example, choreographers may be more preoccupied with exploring the possibilities of technique and movement for movement's sake, and later the pendulum will swing the other way and they will be striving to reform their art by trying to give their works expression and making the technique unobtrusive. The middle of the eighteenth century saw the beginning of just such a period of reform, and the ideas which were then formed and developed were to prove of lasting consequence to the history of ballet. For the first time ballet broke away from opera to exist as an independent art of the theatre. It did so through the development of the *ballet d'action*, by which we mean a ballet in which the dancers themselves convey the plot in dance or mime. As an inevitable consequence, the choreographer was brought into greater prominence than ever before.

The idea that words, whether spoken or sung, can be dispensed with in a ballet originated from the legends about the mimes of the ancient world that cultured people read about in the Greek and Latin classics. Ever since the days of Domenico, dances had been composed that expressed moods and even little scenes, and while Louis XIV was still dancing, a French priest, the Abbé de Pure, wrote a thesis on the need for ballet to do without words. However, there was no real attempt to put these ideas into practice until the eighteenth century.

Then, in 1708, the Duchess of Maine thought of a novel means of entertaining her guests in the little theatre in her château of Sceaux, not far from Paris. She commissioned a composer to set an act of a tragedy to music, and then had it produced without the words, the lines being simply mimed by two dancers from the Opéra, Jean Balon and Françoise Prévost. The experiment was a great success, and the two dancers were so convincing that both they and the audience could not restrain their tears, but the performance seems to have been regarded more as a whim of a great lady than as a serious experiment in choreography.

For another attempt to make use of mime, we must cross the English Channel and enter Drury Lane Theatre to see the work of an English ballet-master called John Weaver. Several years before the Duchess of Maine's fête at Sceaux, Weaver had produced *The Tavern Bilkers*, a burlesque based on mime pieces such as had long been popular in Italy, but his most ambitious work was *The Loves of Mars and Venus*. This was staged in 1717 and is the earliest known ballet which relied on mime and gesture, to the exclusion of the spoken word or song, to convey the action. Thinking that he was reviving a classical form of entertainment, Weaver called it 'the first Trial of this nature that has been made since the reign of Trajan'. The story of how Vulcan cast his net over the lovers to shame them before the other Gods and Goddesses was unfolded in six scenes of expressive dance and mime performed by a cast that included the haughty Louis Dupré and the incomparable Hester Santlow – the first English ballerina of note – as the lovers, and Weaver himself as Vulcan.

During the run of this ballet, the ten-year-old Marie Sallé was dancing at Lincoln's Inn Fields Theatre, within easy reach of Drury Lane. We do not know for certain whether she was able to see Weaver's ballet, but it is very possible that she did so. She had strong views on the importance of expression in ballet which the pantomimes that John Rich produced in Lincoln's Inn Fields must have stimulated and which she maintained throughout her career. At the Paris Opéra, the stronghold of the opera-ballet, she was frustrated because she could not develop her ideas as fully as she wished, and so it was at Drury Lane, in 1734, that she produced *Pigmalion*, in which she discarded the cumbersome pannier that was worn by all ballerinas of that time and appeared instead in a simple muslin dress and with her hair flowing loosely about her shoulders. She performed this miniature masterpiece at her benefit performance, and in later years the great actor David Garrick told Noverre that he remembered people fighting to gain admittance to the theatre that evening.

The ideas that had inspired Weaver and Sallé were soon entering the minds of other choreographers. In Italy danced sketches were quite common, for mime, dance, and acrobatics were all important elements in the popular form of entertainment that was known as the *commedia dell'arte*. Antonio Rinaldi, called Fossano, the teacher of Barberina, married a well-known Harlequin's daughter and was very familiar with the *commedia dell'arte* tradition. He produced a pantomime dance called *Le Bouffon* which he and Barberina danced in Paris in 1739, and in the seventeen-forties staged several comic ballets in St Petersburg. At about the same time – between 1738 and 1761 – Jean-François De Hesse was producing a series of ballet-pantomimes, also deriving from the *commedia dell'arte*, at the Théâtre Italien in Paris. On a more ambitious scale, but owing very little, if anything at all, to the influence of the *commedia dell'arte*, was the work of Franz Hilferding, who was staging mime versions of tragedies and dramas in Vienna in the seventeen-forties and fifties.

Hilferding's pupil, Gaspara Angiolini, held his master in the greatest respect. So much so, indeed, that he became embroiled in a violent quarrel with Noverre, whose claim to have originated the *ballet d'action* roused him to anger. These two choreographers were not really in opposite camps. Both were in fact striving towards the same end, to make ballet a theatrical entertainment capable of profound dramatic meaning. It was only in detail that they differed. The question of the *ballet d'action*'s origin was a minor matter, and Noverre did not dispute Angiolini's championship of Hilferding's claim. More fundamental was their disagreement over the application of the three unities to ballet and the issue of a printed synopsis.

The three unities were rules for the construction of plays which laid down that there should be a single plot, that this should be enacted without change of scenery, and that the action should take place within the space of a single day. Noverre contended that these rules did not apply to ballet, and we can see today that he was correct in disregarding a ridiculous convention. On the other point at issue, however, we may favour Angiolini's point of view. Noverre was in the habit of distributing printed scenarios of his ballets, which Angiolini thought was wrong because a good ballet should be able to tell its own story.

Angiolini, who was an excellent musician, appreciated the importance of the score, and in his early days as ballet-master in Vienna, he was fortunate to enjoy the collaboration of Gluck. Their first ballet together was *Don Juan*, produced in 1761, whose score still has the power to move us today and was used again by Fokine in 1936. Other ballets followed, and Angiolini played a part in the triumph of Gluck's *Orfeo* by arranging the delightful ballet of the Elysian Fields. Later, Angiolini enjoyed successes in St Petersburg and Moscow. Like Weaver and Noverre, he took the Roman mimes as his model, and in *Don Juan*, which he claimed to be the first ballet of its kind, he aimed at making the music replace the declamation that accompanied the gestures of these old mimes. Of course no one had a very clear idea of what the art of these Greek and Roman mimes was like, but the sort of ballet that emerged was a closer synthesis of music and movement than anything that had been produced before. In this and his later ballets, Angiolini showed that he had a sure judgement for choosing a story that could be expressed in easily understandable mime, and a great gift of extracting the maximum effect by the way in which he set gestures to music.

Jean-Georges Noverre enjoyed a much wider reputation than Angiolini, and his place in history is more important because of his influence on other choreographers and because of his writings. His *Letters on Dancing and Ballets*, which have been translated into several languages, are one of the greatest classics in the literature of ballet. The celebrated Noverre, as he was called in his day, was half Swiss and half French, a Protestant by faith, and a few years older than Angiolini. He studied dancing in Paris, and the great Dupré, whom Casanova had seen dancing, masked and bewigged, was one of his teachers. It was no doubt during these early years that Noverre began to see the pointlessness of many of the conventions that hidebound French ballet. He soon began to be noticed by people that mattered. In Berlin as a young man he amused Frederick the Great with his imitations of leading ballerinas and told racy stories to Voltaire who playfully tweaked his ear at the more salacious passages.

His early efforts as a choreographer in the French provinces were so successful that before he was thirty he obtained the support of Madame de Pompadour to apply for the post of ballet-master at the Paris Opéra. His application was turned down, but he consoled himself with an engagement at the Opéra-Comique, where in 1754, he produced his famous Chinese ballet, with scenery and costumes by François Boucher. Things Chinese were all the rage just then, though it was not fashion that drew Paris flocking to see this ballet, but the overall effect of the stage picture, created by Noverre's imaginative and varied choreography and the superb scenery and costumes, all of which went to make up an atmosphere that was really suggestive of the East. In short, it marked a great stride towards our modern conception of what a ballet should be.

The success of this ballet prompted David Garrick, who was married to a dancer, to engage Noverre to bring a company to Drury Lane the following year. It was an unlucky moment, for England and France were on the verge of the Seven Years War and passions were running high among the people of London. Garrick tried to avert a disaster by putting out that Noverre was Swiss, but the mob was not deceived and, despite the presence of George III, the Chinese ballet was performed to a pandemonium of cat-calls and shouts. This was nothing to the riots that broke out on later nights, and Garrick was forced to withdraw the ballet. This unpleasant experience was compensated for Noverre by his friendship with Garrick, who held the choreographer in the highest esteem and called him 'the Shakespeare of the dance'.

Noverre wrote his *Letters* when he was in his thirties, and although he revised them later on, he did not fundamentally alter the ideas he had originally put to paper. They were first printed in Lyon, and published in 1760 both there and in Stuttgart, where he went that same year with increased prestige to produce ballets for the Duke of Württemberg. In Stuttgart Noverre was given the opportunities he must have dreamed of. He was allowed to build up a company of more than fifty dancers; the great *danseur noble*, Gaétan Vestris, came from Paris each year as guest artist; and his ballets were given an equal prominence to the operas. During his seven years in Stuttgart Noverre produced many ballets which he was later to revive elsewhere. One of the most popular was *Medea and Jason*, in which the part of Medea was superbly danced and acted by an English ballerina, Mlle Nency. Nency was a pupil of Noverre, who produced many other fine dancers, including Charles Le Picq, who started in the *corps de ballet* at Stuttgart and was to become one of the greatest *danseurs nobles* of his time.

From Stuttgart, Noverrre went to Vienna, where yet more honours awaited him. Here he produced a succession of epic ballets that marked the peak of his career as a choreographer. Here, too, he collaborated with Gluck by stepping in at the right moment in the production of the opera *Alceste*. Finding the poor composer throwing his wig on to the floor in desperation because he could not make the chorus move as he wanted, Noverre suggested concealing the singers in the wings while dancers mimed the action – an idea that Diaghilev was to use in his production of *Le Coq d'Or* on the eve of the First World War.

Noverre was never really very happy in Vienna, and shortly after his famous quarrel with Angiolini, he left to take up the post of ballet-master at the Paris Opéra, which he had long coveted. This he looked upon as the crowning achievement of his career, but he was soon to be disillusioned. Regarded there as an outsider, he incurred from the outset the enmity of Maximilien Gardel, who considered that the post should have been his by right of succession, because he had been assistant ballet-master before. Consequently, although Noverre staged a number of successful ballets both at the Opéra and at the court of Louis XVI and Marie Antoinette, conditions became more and more difficult for him. He found a sympathizer in the young Mozart, who came to Paris to compose the score for Noverre's ballet *Les Petits Riens* and was disgusted to find that the Opéra added six 'wretched old French airs' to his music. The intrigues against Noverre were strengthened by the hostility of the Opéra's leading ballerina, Madeleine Guimard, and in a short time he yielded to this pressure and tendered his resignation.

London was the scene of his last triumphs. Then came the French Revolution. Ageing and impoverished, he returned to France to live out his last years in a busy retirement. When he was not pottering in his garden, he was occupied in augmenting his *Letters* or paying a visit to Paris to resume touch with the ballet . . . and to be shocked, as old men are inclined to be, by the new trends.

His work had not been in vain. Although none of his ballets have been performed for over a hundred and fifty years, we are still greatly in his debt. This is because, in his *Letters*, he set down principles for choreographers to follow which are as valid today as they were when first written. He stressed that a ballet must have a unity, that feats of technique directed towards displaying a dancer's virtuosity should be avoided, and that everything should contribute towards expressing the ballet's theme. This should be done, he said, by means of movement which was natural and easily understood and which was tailored to the music in much the same way as the words of a song fit the melody.

By expressing these ideas so clearly, Noverre paved the way for the reform of ballet that is associated with his name. Before his time the choreographer had often been rather a shadowy figure in the background. Now, with ballet accepted as an independent art of the theatre, the choreographer emerged as the presiding genius of a ballet's production – an artist in his own right.

Only one ballet has survived in anything like its original state from the age of great choreographers that preceded the Romantic ballet of the nineteenth century. This is Galeotti's *The Whims of Cupid and the Ballet-master*, which has remained in the repertory of the Royal Theatre, Copenhagen, ever since it was created there in 1786, and has more recently been revived at the Paris Opéra. Galeotti, who was a pupil of Angiolini and may also have come under the influence of Noverre, worked in Copenhagen for forty years and, as ballet-master and teacher, first built the Royal Danish Ballet into a great company.

France continued to play a leading part in the development of ballet, and produced many distinguished choreographers. At the Opéra, a succession of important ballets were produced by the brothers Gardel. Maximilien died young, but Pierre continued to exercise an almost despotic sway until the eighteen-twenties. His best works were based on classical legend, and one of them, *Psyche*, was performed at the Opéra more than five hundred times, a record that has since been surpassed only once, by *Coppélia*.

Jean Dauberval, while he produced none of his ballets at the Opéra, was to have a much greater influence on the next generation of choreographers than Pierre Gardel. He opened up new possibilities by producing ballets about ordinary people, and was a master in handling amusing or sentimental themes. 'I am not content with just pleasing the eye,' he once said. 'I want to interest the heart.' One of his ballets, *La Fille Mal Gardée*, is still performed today, though with music and choreography dating from a later period. This ballet was first performed at Bordeaux, an active centre of ballet where Dauberval held the post of ballet-master, just before the French Revolution.

Dauberval's successor at Bordeaux, Jean-Baptiste Blache, also had a bent for comic ballets, one of which alone, *Les Meuniers*, brought him a fortune which he no doubt needed to help support his enormous family of thirty-two children. Returning to Paris, we find working at the Opéra early in the nineteenth century Louis Milon, who was particularly adept at arranging sentimental ballets. *Nina* was his masterpiece, and it contained a mad scene – a forerunner of the famous mad scene in *Giselle* – which Émilie Bigottini mimed so affectingly that spectators often watched her with tears in their eyes.

Dramatic expression was the main object of the great Italian choreographer, Salvatore Viganò. His early ballets were light works after the manner of his teacher, Dauberval, but as he matured he emerged as a choreographer with original ideas of his own. Stendhal, the French writer, had an unbounded admiration for him, comparing him with Shakespeare as a genius of the theatre. For one of his ballets, *The Creatures of Prometheus*, which he produced in Vienna in 1801, Beethoven composed his only ballet score. Viganò's greatest ballets were staged at the Scala, Milan, where he had the freedom and opportunity to work out his ideas, and was helped by having the collaboration of one of the greatest scenic designers of all time, Sanquirico. Viganò was a brilliant musician, and his principal aim was to present a mimed drama in which the action was expressed by gestures and facial expressions in strict time with the music. His ideal was to dispense with the traditional ensemble dances and *pas de deux* and concentrate entirely on the drama, but in only one of his ballets, *The Titans*, did he attempt this. As a choreographer, Viganò was incredibly patient and painstaking. Once he spend a whole morning relentlessly rehearsing eighty dancers in a ten-bar passage until he was wholly satisfied with the result. When he died in 1821 – his death brought on through continuing to rehearse while ill with pleurisy – his admirer Stendhal, realizing that genius such as his cannot be passed on, wrote: 'It was a new art that died with this great man.'

39

Several choreographers working in Italy, including Gaetano Gioja and the Frenchman Louis Henry, were strongly influenced by Viganò's theories but they did not dare to exclude the dance altogether from their ballets, as Viganò would have done. As a result, Italian ballet tended to degenerate into as hybrid a form as the French opera-ballet of old, sometimes with mimes acting the story and dancers coming on just to perform the *pas*. As we shall see in the next chapter, the inspiration for the great period of the Romantic Ballet was to come largely from France.

With Viganò we are in fact almost at the threshold of the Romantic Ballet, but there remains one other important choreographer to note, Charles Didelot. Schooled in the French tradition – he studied under Noverre, Dauberval, and Auguste Vestris – Didelot spent most of his working years in St Petersburg, although his most famous ballet, *Flore et Zéphire* was first produced in London. During the years he spent in St Petersburg, he produced many successful works on themes taken from a great variety of sources. One of these, *The Prisoner in the Caucasus*, was based on a poem by Pushkin, who said there was more poetry to be found in Didelot's ballets than in all the French literature of the time. Didelot had a great sense of period style, and following the precepts of Noverre, he subordinated everything to the ballet's theme. His choreography was particularly notable for the originality and beauty of the groups, which were sometimes suggested by well-known paintings or pieces of sculpture, and he made imaginative use of stage effects, being the first choreographer to have groups of dancers fly by means of wires. He was also a superb teacher. He reorganized the school at St Petersburg, and produced many fine Russian dancers.

So far we have dealt almost exclusively in this chapter with choreographers, but the period we are concerned with – from 1750 to 1820 – was rich too in dancers. While the conception of ballet was being brought much closer to our idea of it today, advances were being made in technique and costume was becoming freer. The ridiculous practice of wearing masks was finally abandoned in the seventeen-seventies, and the panniers and the wigs and the Roman-style costumes had all disappeared by the time the French Revolution broke out. When we reach the turn of the century, ballerinas were wearing costumes that allowed them the freedom of movement they required to perform the newly introduced technical feats such as pirouettes, which women were now performing – an innovation introduced by the German ballerina, Anne Heinel. Another significant change was the disappearance of the heeled shoe, but the development that sprang from this belongs to the next chapter.

Standing out like giants among the dancers of this time are the two Vestrises, Gaétan and Auguste, father and son, who between them dominated the Paris Opéra ballet for over fifty years – from the time of La Pompadour, through the strife of the French Revolution, into the stirring days of Napoleon. Gaétan Vestris followed the great Dupré, his teacher, in the noble style of dancing – one of the three categories into which the dancers of the Paris Opéra were then classified according to their physique and style, the others being the demi-caractère and the comic styles. He too was called the God of the Dance – or *'le Dio de la Danse'*, in imitation of his strong Italian accent – and his supremacy was never seriously challenged.

There was only one other dancer whom he acknowledged to be superior to himself, and that was his son Auguste, whose style was the demi-caractère. 'The explanation is simple,' he added. 'Gaétan Vestris is his father, an advantage which Nature has denied me.' Auguste was equally vain. 'In Europe,' he once said, 'there are only three great men – myself, Voltaire, and the King of Prussia.' And when a lady apologized for stepping on his foot in a crowd and asked if he was hurt, she received the annihilating reply: 'No, madame, but you have nearly put the whole of Paris into mourning for a fortnight.'

Auguste Vestris's career was extraordinarily long. He was the darling of the public during the old régime, when Kings of France lived at Versailles, and this we can well imagine as we look at the print that was published in London in 1781, showing him apparently spinning round in a brilliant *pirouette à la seconde* with his hat in his hand. Here he is in the very prime of life, when he was famed for his astonishing facility in turns and jumps. But alas, like many another, he danced for longer than he ought. When he eventually retired as a dancer he devoted himself to teaching and formed several excellent dancers of the Romantic period. Once, in his seventies, he emerged from retirement to dance a stately gavotte with Taglioni, and he died the year after *Giselle* was first produced, remembered with amused affection by the nickname of 'Grandpapa Zephyr' that suggested past glories which were already half forgotten.

In the later years of his stage career, Auguste Vestris had to contend with the wonderful talent of a much younger dancer, Louis Duport, who moved with the ease and grace of a young cat. Duport enjoyed many triumphs in Russia, and we catch a glimpse of him in Tolstoy's great novel, *War and Peace*, when Natasha visits the Opera and watches him 'leaping very high and making rapid movements in the air with his feet'. 'Isn't Duport ravishing!' her companion murmured, as the audience were shouting his name.

Although this was an age when the male dancer was king, there were many famous ballerinas too: Anne Heinel, a powerfully built dancer from Germany who became the wife of Gaétan Vestris . . . Geltrude Rossi, the wife of Le Picq and a great dramatic dancer . . . Giovanna Bacelli, who was painted by Reynolds and Gainsborough, and whose statue is to be seen at Knole . . . Madeleine Guimard, who danced for many years at the Paris Opéra . . . Théodore, Dauberval's wife and the original Lise in *La Fille Mal Gardée* . . . the lovely Maria Medina, a Spaniard who married Viganò . . . Marie Gardel, the wife of Pierre Gardel and the star of many of his ballets . . . Émilie Bigottini, Napoleon's favourite dancer and a very affecting actress . . . Maria Danilova, a pupil of Didelot who was showing the most exceptional promise in St Petersburg when she died at the age of seventeen . . . and many others besides.

But gifted though they were, these ballerinas were often overshadowed by the brilliance of a Vestris or a Duport. The era of male supremacy, however, was nearing its term. For we are now standing at the threshold of the Romantic Ballet, which was to see the ballerina dazzle her male partner into oblivion so completely that he was to fall out of favour almost everywhere until Diaghilev came many years later to restore the balance.

CHAPTER FOUR

The Romantic Ballet

THE Romantic Ballet is probably the most familiar and appealing of all periods in ballet history. Not only have many books and articles been written about it, but its wonderful galaxy of ballerinas come alive for us in the superb coloured lithographs of the time, and some of its ballets are still performed, as fresh as ever, though nowadays touched with fragrant old-world charm. The best known of these is, of course, *Giselle*, which is danced today by companies all over the world, but there also exists a wonderful collection of ballets by Bournonville – *Napoli*, *La Sylphide*, *Kermesse in Bruges*, *A Folk Tale*, and others – which have been faithfully preserved in Copenhagen for a century and more by the Royal Danish Ballet.

We already feel at home when we reach the Romantic Ballet, not only because we know some of the ballets that date from that period, but because costume styles, methods of presentation, and dance technique have drawn much nearer to our standards of today. Dancers' costumes, as we have seen, had become very much simpler around 1800, but as we approach the middle of the nineteenth century – in the early years of Queen Victoria's reign – the ballerina's skirt follows the trend in women's everyday fashions and becomes more bell-shaped. This style of costume is still used in many ballets today, and we sometimes call the bell-shaped skirt that reaches to the knee or below a 'Romantic tutu'. The stage picture – the ballet as seen by the audience – has also come closer to what the public of today is accustomed to, and the introduction of gas lighting, the practice of bringing the curtain down between the scenes and lowering the house lights during the performance, and other factors as well, all helped to produce a greater illusion than ever before.

The Romantic Ballet is given its name because it is a part of the Romantic movement which breathed new vitality into every form of art in the early nineteenth century. This movement arose at a time when the social order was in a state of change and new ideas were bubbling up to the surface of men's minds. A new wealthy class, which had grown rich through the expansion of industry and commerce, was taking its place in society, and people were beginning to view many problems in a different light. The force of the new ideas of liberty and equality, for example, showed itself in the violence of the French Revolution, and the new ideas that lay behind the Romantic movement in art were just as potent and effective in their different ways.

Art was in great need of reform, for around 1800 many artists were so obsessed with classicism that they often paid more attention to the form of their work than to its content. Consequently, although their technique might have been above reproach, their work tended to be cold and somewhat lifeless. The Romantic movement was to a large extent a revolt against this obsession with form. Writers, painters, musicians, and artists of all kinds began to seek fresh sources of inspiration and to express themselves in different ways. The works of these artists, whom we collectively term the Romantic school to distinguish them from the Classical school, were full of feeling and warmth. This new spirit infused the writings of Byron, Scott, and Hugo, the music of Berlioz, Chopin, and Mendelssohn, and the paintings of Delacroix and Corot, and in due time it found its way into ballet too.

The great significance of the Romantic Ballet lay in the fact that ballets became more poetic and appealed more directly and more profoundly to the emotions of the audience than they had done in earlier times. This was largely brought about by the introduction of a more poetic style of dancing which we associate particularly with the name of Marie Taglioni, and by the way in which choreographers, assisted by scenarists, composers, and designers, enabled this style to be displayed to the best advantage. Choreographers were becoming increasingly aware of the importance of atmosphere, whether in producing the supernatural scenes that were so popular at that time or in placing their ballets in some faraway land or in another period, and designers and musicians were also working towards the same end. Scenery was becoming more complicated in construction and more realistic in design, and lighting effects undreamed of in earlier times were now possible through the introduction of gas lighting. The general illusion was further heightened by the music, which was becoming much more descriptive, as we can hear for ourselves by comparing Adolphe Adam's score for *Giselle* – one of the finest examples of Romantic ballet music – even with Gluck's *Don Juan*, which was unusually descriptive for its period.

Perhaps the most significant change that we notice in ballets of the Romantic period is in the choice of themes. During the eighteen-thirties, a fertile new source was discovered in legends about fantastic or supernatural creatures such as sylphides, wilis, peris, naiads and their like. The fashion changed so rapidly and radically that the Gods of Mount Olympus and the heroes of ancient legend, who had been such favourite figures only a few years before, were banished from the ballet stage almost overnight. Supernatural scenes, however, form only one side of the picture of the Romantic Ballet, for at the same time rustic scenes, often set in some exotic land, were very popular and formed the setting for touches of 'local colour' such as stylized dances from Spain or Poland or a glamorized East.

In several of the great ballets of the period – for instance, in *La Sylphide* and *Giselle* – these two aspects, the real and the unreal, the earthly and the ethereal, exist side by side. As a result, ballet became richer because both these aspects required different styles of dancing if they were to be properly contrasted with each other. For the scenes of real life the style tended to be more earthbound, or *terre à terre*, and the choreographer usually made much use of intricate and rapid steps to which the adjective *tacqueté* was given. The supernatural scenes, on the other hand, required a choreography that was more poetic in feeling and based much more on steps of elevation, and a style that was termed *ballonné*.

An important element in Romantic choreography, particularly in these supernatural scenes, was the use of *pointe* work. The discovery of *pointe* work is one of the most important developments in dance technique in the whole history of ballet. It was probably an inevitable consequence of the discarding of the heeled shoe towards the end of the eighteenth century, for rising on to the tips of the toes is a natural expression of lightness, and what was more natural than to try and carry this to its logical conclusion by reducing the contact with the ground to the barest minimum. *Pointe* work evolved gradually, and we cannot say that any one ballerina invented it. One of the first to rise on her *pointes* was Geneviève Gosselin of the Paris Opéra, who died at the peak of her career in 1818; there is evidence that the Russian dancer Istomina may have accomplished it at about the same time, and probably other ballerinas did so too. But it was only during the eighteen-twenties that *pointe* work began to be seriously developed, mainly in Italy, as a means of virtuosity. It finally emerged as a necessary part of the ballerina's vocabulary when Marie Taglioni showed how it could be used to enhance her grace and convey an illusion of weightlessness – a quality that was a wonderful asset to choreographers who were introducing the supernatural element into their ballets.

The development of *pointe* work was only one indication of the radical transformation that had taken place in the technique of ballet since the days of Noverre. Another was the perfection of the pirouette, which in the early nineteenth century could be performed with a finish that was never seen fifty years before. This transformation of technique had been brought about through improved teaching methods which culminated in that of Carlo Blasis, who in 1820 codified the technique of his time in his *Elementary, Theoretical and Practical Treatise of the Art of the Dance*. From this book, which he wrote at the age of twenty-four, stem many of today's methods of ballet teaching.

Blasis was a remarkable man. As his prolific writings show,

he was an expert on many subjects, but his great importance in the history of ballet is due to his work as a teacher. In 1837 he became head of the Imperial Dancing Academy, the ballet school attached to La Scala, Milan, where he turned out many brilliant dancers who went out to conquer audiences not only in Italy but all over the world. His fame was such that many established stars, such as Fanny Cerrito and Lucile Grahn, went to study under him. Blasis's method has been passed from teacher to teacher right down to our time. Enrico Cecchetti – who taught Pavlova, Nijinsky, Lifar, Fornaroli, de Valois, and many other famous dancers of the present century – was himself taught by one of Blasis's best pupils, and Carlotta Zambelli, who taught several generations of dancers at the Paris Opéra, was also a product of the Scala school and in her classes uses *enchaînements* that had been invented by Blasis himself a century before. In this way the work of Blasis lives on, and has become the very backbone of today's classic ballet technique.

During the period of the Romantic Ballet, the main centre of ballet activity was the Paris Opéra, where *La Sylphide* and *Giselle* were first produced and where most of the greatest ballerinas of the time built up their reputations. The old order was already fast disappearing there in the eighteen-twenties. Pierre Gardel had at last retired and the leading choreographer was Jean Aumer, whose ballets included *La Somnambule* – the plot of which was to be used again for Bellini's well-known opera – and a version of *The Sleeping Beauty*.

In 1831 the Opéra became a private enterprise, and its new Director, Dr Véron, was so successful in making it popular and fashionable, not only among the aristocracy, but among the rising middle class, that after five years he was able to retire with a fortune. His innovations included the introduction of the star system and allowing the more important subscribers to go backstage to the Foyer de la Danse and pass the time during the intervals talking and flirting with the dancers. The Foyer de la Danse became a kind of social institution in Paris, and remained so until not long before the Second World War.

Dr Véron promoted Marie Taglioni over the heads of the other leading dancers to the position of star ballerina, and presented her in a number of ballets by her father, Filippo Taglioni. The most famous of these were the Ballet of the Nuns in the opera *Robert the Devil*, which inaugurated the cult for the supernatural, the poetic *La Sylphide*, and *The Daughter of the Danube*. In 1834 Véron stimulated the public's interest still further by engaging another ballerina, Fanny Elssler, between whom and Taglioni there arose much the same sort of rivalry that had divided Paris into two camps in the days of Camargo and Sallé. Elssler was to shine in ballets by two other choreographers, Jean Coralli who produced *The Devil on Two Sticks* and *The Gipsy* for her, and Joseph Mazilier who provided her with another triumph in *La Tarentule*.

Although Dr Véron's successors at the Opéra were financially not so fortunate as he, they continued the tradition of ballet with works such as *Giselle* and *Le Diable à Quatre* in the eighteen-forties and *The Corsair* in the fifties, and Taglioni and Elssler were in turn followed by a succession of other stars – Carlotta Grisi, Fanny Cerrito, Carolina Rosati, Amalia Ferraris, and one exceptionally talented French girl among them, the ill-fated Emma Livry.

London at this time was a particularly profitable field for dancers, and for a time seriously challenged the supremacy of Paris. Ballet had been given at the King's Theatre – or Her Majesty's, as it was called when Queen Victoria came to the throne – since the middle of the eighteenth century, and its popularity reached its peak in the eighteen-forties when Benjamin Lumley was manager. Lumley had the discernment and the good fortune to engage as his ballet-master Jules Perrot, probably the greatest choreographer of the time, who produced there a number of important ballets which told strong dramatic stories. Perrot was not only a brilliant arranger of dances and crowd scenes, but he also knew, better than any other choreographer of his time, how to use the dance to help express the action. Some of his *pas d'action*, such as the fascination dance in *Alma* and the shadow dance in *Ondine*, were vital passages in the unfolding of the plot. Perhaps the most brilliant ballet he staged in London was *La Esmeralda*, which was based on Victor Hugo's novel *Notre Dame de Paris*. This ballet, which was first produced in 1844, brilliantly caught the atmosphere of medieval Paris, and Carlotta Grisi, and later Fanny Elssler, both excelled in the role of the gipsy heroine. *Ondine*, in which Cerrito had one of her greatest parts, and *Catarina*, which was produced for Lucile Grahn, were hardly less successful.

But Perrot's work for Lumley was not confined to grand ballets such as these. He also produced four all-star *divertissements*, which showed how perfectly he understood the styles of the great ballerinas with whom he worked. It was Lumley's policy to engage several ballerinas for the same season. At first, if more than one were appearing on the same evening, they were presented in separate ballets, but in 1843 Queen Victoria asked that Fanny Elssler and Fanny Cerrito should dance a *pas de deux* together at a Command Performance. It proved to be the sensation of the season, and two years later, having no less than four ballerinas at his disposal – Taglioni, Cerrito, Grisi, and Grahn – Lumley announced the *Pas de Quatre*.

This, the first and most famous of Perrot's all-star *divertissements*, was perhaps the most sublime ballet that was produced throughout the whole of the Romantic period. It has now become a legend, and in our time both Keith Lester and Anton Dolin have been inspired to recreate it, necessarily with different choreography but with the original music, which was discovered in a piano version in the British Museum. Its first production in 1845 was almost prevented by a clash of personalities. On the very morning it was to be given, Cerrito and Carlotta Grisi had a violent quarrel over the order of their *variations*, each considering that her *variation* should follow the other's. Tempers ran so high that Perrot fled in despair to Lumley's office. Happily Lumley was master of the situation. 'The question,' he said calmly, 'must be decided by the public ... Let the oldest take her unquestionable right to the enviable position.' When Perrot returned to announce this decision, the ballerinas looked embarrassed and the dispute was forgotten.

Unfortunately the popularity of ballet at Her Majesty's Theatre waned rapidly after the appearance in 1847 of Jenny Lind, the Swedish Nightingale, who was very largely responsible for restoring the vogue for opera. In a very short time ballet was all but banished from the opera house in London, and during the second half of the nineteenth century it was to survive mainly in the great music halls of the capital.

Ballet was more fortunate in Italy, Russia, and Denmark, where companies were firmly established with their schools in the great opera houses. In Italy, the tradition of choreography set by Viganò was continued by Louis Henry, Antonio Cortesi, Antonio Monticini and others who produced works on a lavish scale with strong and complex plots, often acted by mimes while the dancers were introduced only in the *divertissements*. Meanwhile, Russia was consolidating a tradition which, while remaining Russian in spirit, was, in St Petersburg, distinctly French in flavour. From the mid-century onwards a series of important French choreographers were permanently engaged there: first Perrot, then Saint-Léon, and finally Marius Petipa. Ballet was also growing in importance in Moscow, where, in the early eighteen-sixties, Carlo Blasis, then an old man, went as choreographer and teacher. Another offshoot of the French school was to be found in the Royal Danish Ballet at Copenhagen, which was dominated by August Bournonville from 1830, with a few intervals, until his death in 1877. Bournonville had studied dancing in Paris under Auguste Vestris, and the 'Bournonville style' of Danish dancers today is fundamentally the French style of a hundred years ago. He was an excellent dancer as well as a great choreographer and a fine teacher, and consequently his ballets, unlike those of many of his contemporaries, contained plenty of opportunities for male dancers.

In addition to these important centres of ballet, there were many other places where choreographers and dancers were active: Berlin, where Marie Taglioni's brother, Paul Taglioni, a fine choreographer, produced many ballets, Vienna, Lisbon, Budapest, Warsaw, and countless smaller cities and towns. And across the Atlantic, in a fast expanding United States, the first American dancers were emerging: Mary Ann Lee, the first American to dance *Giselle*, Augusta Maywood, and George Washington Smith, to name but three.

The Romantic Ballet was wonderfully rich in ballerinas, and their brilliance, which was enhanced by the exciting discovery of the *pointe*, quite eclipsed all but a few outstanding male dancers. Acknowledged as the queen of them all was Marie Taglioni, whose name was mentioned with a tone of reverent regret by people who had seen her dance, for full half a century after she retired. She came to Paris, virtually unknown, in 1827 and quite revolutionized the style of dancing at the Opéra. The other dancers there were forced to emulate her smooth movements, and a new verb – to taglionize – was coined. Although she raised *pointe* work from a feat to an art, she was in no sense a virtuoso. She was a lyrical dancer, moving through the air with long floating bounds and alighting with hardly a sound. It might be said that she brought poetry to an art that, before her, had never risen above the level of prose. Her father, Filippo Taglioni, was her teacher, and he was so ruthless in his demands that at the end of a two-hour lesson, she was often almost unconscious with fatigue and had to be undressed, sponged and dressed again before she revived.

It was her father too who arranged many of the ballets in which she danced, and together they formed an almost perfect partnership, for he would not be regarded so highly as a choreographer had she not gained some of her greatest triumphs in his ballets, while she, for her part, may never have found another choreographer who so completely understood her qualities. Her ethereal style expressed the demands of Romanticism to perfection and encouraged the introduction of themes based on the supernatural. Their first essay of this kind was the Ballet of the Nuns in the opera *Robert the Devil*, which was produced at the Paris Opéra in 1831. The scene of the lapsed nuns called forth from their tombs to dance in the moonlit ruins of their cloister – the set was one of the master-pieces of the great scene designer of the time, Ciceri – caught the imagination of the public, and *La Sylphide* followed almost as a natural consequence. This ballet told of a mysterious crea-ture of the air, a sylphide, who falls in love with a Scotsman and comes between him and his fiancée, only to die at his hands when he places about her shoulders a scarf, over which an evil witch has cast her spell. It was a classic example of mixing the worlds of reality and fantasy in a ballet, and nine nine years later *Giselle* was to be created in the same form. *La Sylphide*, in Taglioni's version, has long been forgotten, but Bournonville's version of the same ballet, produced four years later to a different score, is still performed by the Royal Danish Ballet, and in 1946 Victor Gsovsky attempted a reconstruction of the ballet with the original score by Schneitzhoeffer for the Ballets des Champs-Élysées.

Marie Taglioni danced the role of the Sylphide to the end of her career, becoming identified with it in much the same way as Pavlova with the Dying Swan. But she danced other types of role as well, and one of her triumphs was in a stylized Spanish dance called the *Gitana*. She was worshipped as no other ballerina before her or in her time, not only in Paris, but in London, St Petersburg, and many other cities besides. The stern and unbending Tsar Nicholas I hardly missed a perform-ance when she was in Russia, and the balletomanes of St Petersburg carried their adulation so far that they held a banquet and consumed a pair of her ballet shoes cooked and served with a special sauce. Her last triumphs took place in London, in two of Perrot's all-star *divertissements*, the *Pas de Quatre* and *The Judgment of Paris*. Though she was dancing with ballerinas of the very top class and a generation younger than herself, her supremacy remained unchallenged.

Taglioni's greatest rival was the Viennese dancer Fanny Elssler, and their styles could hardly have been more different. Théophile Gautier, the Romantic poet who was also a great lover and critic of ballet, described Taglioni as a Christian dancer and Elssler as a pagan dancer. While Taglioni's style was poetic and ethereal, Elssler danced with passion and developed into a dancer-actress of great power. Her most famous dance was the *Cachucha*, a stylized Spanish dance which she performed in the ballet *The Devil on Two Sticks*. After rising to fame at the Paris Opéra, she crossed the Atlantic in 1840 to become the first great ballerina to dance in America. Her triumphs there were fabulous. The President and his Cabinet gave her an official audience, and when she was dancing in Washington, Congress adjourned because most of its members were at the theatre anyway and there was no hope of obtaining a quorum. She delayed her return to Europe long after she was due to resume her duties at the Paris Opéra. To appear there again was consequently out of the question, but there were many other stages open to her. In London she gave some electrifying performances in *Giselle* and *La Esmeralda*, and she became a great favourite at La Scala, Milan, until the year of revolution, 1848, when she suffered through being Austrian and was hissed off the stage by a hot-headed audience of Italian patriots.

Within the space of a few years the Paris Opéra lost both Taglioni and Elssler, but their place was soon filled in the hearts of the ballet-going public by a young Italian dancer called Carlotta Grisi. Within a few months of her début at the Opéra in 1841, Carlotta created the title-role in *Giselle*, a role which ballerinas ever since have looked upon much as actors regard Hamlet. She had captivated Théophile Gautier, who was never to tire of writing of her charms and who conceived the original idea of *Giselle*, based upon the German legend of the wilis, the restless spirits of girls who have died on their wedding eve. In the ballet Giselle is a peasant girl who, in the first act, loses her reason and dies after learning that her lover has betrayed her, and, in the second act, becoming a wili, is commanded by her queen to lure her lover to his death, a command that is defeated by the coming of dawn when the wilis' power is broken. Like *La Sylphide*, the plot of *Giselle* is worked out on the two planes of the real and the supernatural, and it has come down to us today in the version as performed in St Petersburg at the end of the century. In the original Paris production, Perrot had arranged Carlotta's dances, but the rest of the choreography was by Jean Coralli, whose name alone appeared on the bill. Gautier wrote the scenario of another ballet for Carlotta, called *La Péri*, for which Coralli arranged the choreography, and she also created the title-role in Perrot's great dramatic ballet *La Esmeralda*.

One of the few internationally famous ballerinas of the period to make her name outside the Paris Opéra was Fanny Cerrito. She was London's special favourite, and commanded a staunch body of admirers among the occupants of the omnibus boxes that flanked the front of the stage at Her Majesty's Theatre. Her great roles were in *Alma*, *Ondine*, with its famous Shadow Dance (an idea which Frederick Ashton has incorporated in his own *Ondine*), and *La Vivandière*, and she appeared in every one of Perrot's all-star *divertissements*. The secret of her attraction lay in her languorous feminine appeal, her suppleness of movement, and above all her speed and attack. Hans Andersen, among many others, found her irresistible. 'There must be youth,' he wrote, 'and that I found in Cerrito. It was something incomparably beautiful, it was a swallow flight in the dance, a sport of Psyche.' During her early seasons in London she was most carefully chaperoned by her father, a retired soldier of the Napoleonic Wars, who used to identify himself with her triumphs, saying to all who would listen: 'We have danced magnificently tonight.' Cerrito married the dancer and choreographer, Arthur Saint-Léon, who arranged many ballets for her, but they separated after a few years. She was also a choreographer herself, and one of her ballets, *Gemma*, had a scenario by Théophile Gautier and was produced at the Paris Opéra in 1854. Like many of the great dancers of this and every other time, she lived to a great age, surviving all three ballerinas who had danced with her in the *Pas de Quatre*, and dying, aged over ninety, only a few days before the Diaghilev Ballet opened their first season in Paris.

These were the really great ballerinas of the period, but there were many others who attained distinction: Lucile Grahn, a Danish dancer and the youngest of the four who took part in the *Pas de Quatre*; Elena Andreyanova, the first St Petersburg Giselle; Ekaterina Sankovskaya, the Moscow ballerina known as 'the Russian Taglioni' who in her old age became the first teacher of the great theatre producer Stanislavksy; Sofia Fuoco, a pupil of Carlo Blasis and such an astonishing virtuoso of *pointe* work that she was known as '*la pointue*'; Carolina Rosati, who created the leading part in *The Corsair*; Augusta Maywood, an American-born ballerina who had a long and distinguished career in Italy; Amalia Ferraris, who was gifted with a wonderful elevation; and many others who were applauded with enthusiastic fervour in theatres all over Europe.

We have so far hardly glanced at the male dancers, who not only had to contend with these brilliant ballerinas but also an increasing prejudice on the part of the public. The extension of the ballerina's technique through the development of *pointe* work and the fact that men seemingly had no part in the ethereal scenes of sylphides, wilis, and ondines contributed to the male dancer's decline. This decline set in rapidly, for as late as the eighteen-twenties Albert and Paul and other male dancers were still in great favour with the public. The Romantic period possessed fewer good male dancers than any previous age in the history of ballet, and many dancers who might have become outstanding must have been disheartened at the outset by the lack of opportunities given them and by the public's indifference.

A few, however, were able to make their mark. Jules Perrot, in his younger days, bid fair to challenge Taglioni herself, who once, after they had danced a *pas de deux* together, was heard to complain: 'Is it not terrible when a male dancer receives more applause than I!' Bournonville described Perrot as 'a sylph with the wings of a bat', and Gautier called him 'the male Taglioni'. Praise could not have gone further. August Bournonville was another fine dancer, and being a choreographer too, he was in a position to preserve the dignity of the male dancer in Copenhagen to a much greater degree than else-where. In Paris Lucien Petipa, the first Albrecht in *Giselle*, long found favour so far as his opportunities allowed, and Arthur Saint-Léon's phenomenal technique did not go unnoticed.

When we reach the eighteen-fifties, the Romantic Ballet is already losing its force. But before we pass on, one more dancer claims our attention. The tragedy of Emma Livry is more than a reminder of the dangers that dancers had to face in the days of gas lighting. It is made doubly heart-rending by the thought of the wonderful talent that was wasted through one moment of carelessness. She danced for only four years after making her début at the Paris Opéra in no less a role than that of the Sylphide. Such an attempt must have seemed almost impertinently audacious, but she justified it so com-pletely that Marie Taglioni came hurrying from her retirement to produce a ballet for her and resume her career as the Opéra's principal teacher. The ballet was *Le Papillon*, with music by Offenbach, produced in 1860. Two years later Taglioni began work on another ballet for the girl who by then had become her cherished pupil, and of whom she was heard to say: 'I never saw myself dance, but I must have danced like her.' This second ballet was never completed, for while it was still in preparation, Emma Livry brushed too closely to a wing light during a rehearsal, her costume caught fire, and when the flames were finally put out she was most terribly burned. She died of her injuries after eight months of suffering, and the white butterflies which Gautier noticed fluttering above the coffin on its funeral journey seemed to be mourning not only a brilliant young dancer struck down in her prime but a great period of ballet.

CHAPTER FIVE

The Decline of Ballet in the West

So far we have been more concerned with Paris than anywhere else, and we have only given an occasional glance towards far-away Russia – far away indeed in those times, when it took several days to reach St Petersburg (the city which we know today as Leningrad) and still longer to arrive in Moscow. Now, however – in the fifty prosperous years before the First World War of 1914–18 – St Petersburg takes pride of place, supplanting Paris as the main centre of ballet. In St Petersburg alone the art of ballet maintained an equal standing with opera, and at the lovely Maryinsky Theatre, with its huge auditorium decorated in blue and gold, the great Tchaikovsky ballets – *The Sleeping Beauty*, *The Nutcracker*, and *Swan Lake* – were just as important creations as the operas.

Meanwhile, ballet in Western Europe was passing through a period of decline, and not even the brilliant talents of such great ballerinas as Legnani, Zambelli, and Genée could give it back the prestige which it enjoyed in the Romantic period. We must not be misled, however, into believing that there was little activity in Paris and London and Milan during those years, and so, before we turn our attention to Russia, let us see what took place in those cities.

We left Paris in 1863 mourning the death of Emma Livry. Ballet was still very popular then, and that same year a young Russian ballerina called Martha Muravieva made her début at the Opéra in a revival of *Giselle* and Saint-Léon returned to produce a new ballet. Saint-Léon was at that time ballet-master in St Petersburg, but the seasons there only lasted for about six months, and for several years he was able to go every summer to Paris. There he produced *La Source* in 1866 and, four years later, *Coppélia*, which was not only his greatest ballet but his last, for he died, prematurely worn out by illness and overwork, a few months after its first performance.

These two ballets introduced an important composer of ballet music, Léo Delibes, whose wonderful gift of melody is shown at its best in *Coppélia*. The role of the heroine Swanilda is a favourite one with many ballerinas who can combine light comedy with a brilliant and sparkling technique. Swanilda is a village girl whose fiancée is smitten with the charms of a mysterious girl whom he sees sitting reading at a window. He does not realize that it is only a doll made by the old toymaker Dr Coppélius, and the ballet tells how Swanilda and her friends make their way into the workshop and how she fools the old toymaker by taking the doll's place and pretending to come alive. All ends happily, of course, for this is a light ballet, and there is a bright *divertissement* to bring the final curtain down.

Saint-Léon spent such a long time preparing this ballet that the first dancer he chose for the leading part fell ill and a young Italian ballerina called Giuseppina Bozzacchi, who had never appeared in public before, stepped into her shoes. The first performance was given only a few weeks before the outbreak of the Franco-Prussian War, which claimed as one of its victims little Bozzacchi, who died of smallpox during the Siege of Paris, on a cold winter's morning that happened to be her seventeenth birthday.

When *Coppélia* was revived after the war, with the sprightly, birdlike Léontine Beaugrand as Swanilda, we have reached the period which comes alive for us in the paintings and drawings of dancers backstage by Degas and, for those who read French, in Ludovic Halévy's short stories about the Cardinal family. Degas was only interested in the dancers themselves, and, with few exceptions, none of his pictures depict scenes from actual ballets. This is not surprising, for in fact only two ballets have survived out of all that were produced at the Paris Opéra between 1871 and 1909, and these two largely on account of their music. Without Delibes' score, *Sylvia* would probably be a very dull ballet, for its story of one of Diana's nymphs who falls in love with a shepherd contains no real dramatic or human interest. Louis Mérante arranged the choreography for the first performance in 1876, and Rita Sangalli, a brilliant Italian ballerina from Milan, was the first to dance the part of Sylvia. The other ballet that has survived is *The Two Pigeons*, which also had choreography by Mérante. Messager wrote a score that is full of good melodies for that ballet, and the leading role was first danced, in 1886, by Rosita Mauri, a Spanish ballerina. We need only pause to remember two other ballets: Mérante's Breton ballet, *La Korrigane*, to music by Widor, which was created in 1880 and was a favourite for many years, giving Mauri one of her best parts; and *Namouna*, which Lucien Petipa produced in 1882. *Namouna* has not been performed for a long time, but some of Lalo's music for it, which was so advanced for its time that it caused an uproar in the theatre when it was first played, is still heard at the Opéra, where it accompanies Lifar's *Suite en Blanc* (or, as it is called when given by the Cuevas Ballet, *Noir et Blanc*).

The Opéra's greatest star during these years was Carlotta Zambelli. Few careers in ballet can have been so long as hers. More than sixty years separate her début, as a girl of seventeen, in 1894 and her retirement as a teacher in 1955. In her days as a ballerina, she not only possessed a brilliant technique, but interpreted her parts with a delicious wit that the Paris audiences loved. Many ballets were produced for her by Joseph Hansen, Ivan Clustine and Léo Staats, but she is best remembered, by those who saw her dance, for her performances in *Sylvia* – perhaps no other dancer has excelled her in this part – and in *Coppélia*.

During all this time, ballet was being looked upon more and more as a secondary entertainment which filled up the programme after the opera or was inserted in the opera itself as a *divertissement*. The eclipse of the male dancer, which had begun during the Romantic period, continued, and male roles were often taken by women in travesty. That of Frantz in *Coppélia*, for example, was originally played by the beautiful Eugénie Fiocre, who specialized in such parts and whose shapely legs were much admired by the men-about-town of the Second Empire. The Paris Opéra long preserved this tradition in its production of *Coppélia*, and when the role was well played the effect could be very charming. But whereas a travesty role may now be justified in an isolated instance on historical grounds, in those days it was a sign of the virtual exclusion of featured male dancers from the Paris Opéra ballet. There were a few rare exceptions, such as Vasquez and Aveline, but generally the men were only employed for character roles and supporting parts.

The situation in London was no better than in Paris. Her Majesty's Theatre, where there had been so much fine ballet in the eighteen-forties, never possessed a permanently established ballet organization, and consequently, when ballet went out of favour, dancers were usually engaged only for incidental dances in the operas. Having been all but banished from the opera house, ballet then took root in two great music halls, the Alhambra and the Empire in Leicester Square, where it occupied the greater part of the programmes alongside variety acts. In these surroundings ballet flourished and attracted a very large public, but it was a public that was seeking light entertainment and so there was no hope of ballet rising there to any high artistic level.

The Alhambra was the larger of these two music halls, and spectacle always played an important part in its ballets. Transformation scenes and water effects were very popular, and once the audience was sprayed with scent during a ballet. At first there was very little dramatic action in these ballets, but by the nineties ballets with quite complicated plots were being staged. Some, such as Léon Espinosa's *Sleeping Beauty*, were based on fairy-tales and produced at Christmas, some told well-known stories such as *Don Juan*, *Don Quixote*, and *Carmen*, and others had modern settings and contained topical allusions, for the music hall audience above all wanted a show that was up to date. Typical of the last type were the military ballets and the ballets that were staged to celebrate Jubilees, Coronations, International Exhibitions, and other such occasions. The

Alhambra did not stint itself in its ballet department. It maintained a very large *corps de ballet*, consisting almost entirely of girls, and engaged a succession of celebrated choreographers, including Joseph Hansen, Carlo Coppi, and Alfredo Curti, to produce the ballets. The music was generally composed or arranged by the theatre's musical director, and nearly fifty scores were thus provided by George Jacobi in the twenty-six years that he held this position before his retirement in 1898. Neither was expense spared in bringing over star ballerinas, usually from Milan. Emma Bessone, Emma Palladino, Cecilia Cerri, Maria Bordin all became favourites with the audiences there, but the most famous of all was the great Pierina Legnani, who was performing her feat of thirty-two consecutive *fouettés* at the Alhambra before she went to Russia and introduced them first into Petipa's *Cinderella* and then into *Swan Lake*.

The Empire adopted much the same policy as the Alhambra, although, because it was smaller, it could not produce its ballets on so lavish a scale. For many years its ballets were produced by a combination of three people – Katti Lanner as choreographer, Leopold Wenzel as composer, and C. Wilhelm as designer. Wilhelm eventually became the most important partner, and not only designed the costumes, as originally had been his only task, but supervised the entire production, giving the most meticulous attention to the colour schemes. This trio was responsible for the ballets in which Adeline Genée danced during her early years in London.

Genée, a Danish ballerina, was engaged for only six weeks in 1897, the year of Queen Victoria's Diamond Jubilee, but her contract was renewed over and over again, and all through the Edwardian era she was one of the most popular personalities in the London theatre. Her technique was perfect and her timing had to be seen to be believed. She also had an exquisite sense of humour which was perfectly suited to the role of Swanilda in *Coppélia*. Like Zambelli's, her career was a very long one. She retired as a dancer after visiting the United States and Australia, but later played an important part in establishing what is now the Royal Academy of Dancing, and was its first President until 1954.

Italy was still looked upon as the main source of supply of ballerinas, and when an opera house manager needed a new star his first thought was usually of the ballet school of La Scala, Milan. Sangalli, Legnani, and Zambelli all came from that school, where the tradition of Blasis's teaching was observed and the training had been developed to the point of producing dancers capable of performing wonderful feats of virtuosity. It was there that dancers discovered how to perfect those long sequences of *fouettés* with which Bessone and Legnani astonished Russia and which Zambelli introduced to Paris.

The main purpose of this ballet school was to supply the Scala itself with dancers, for ballet was still staged there on the grandest scale. An enormous company of dancers was maintained who were fully employed in the fantastic productions of the choreographer Luigi Manzotti towards the end of the nineteenth century. Manzotti wrote the scenarios of his ballets as well as producing them, and often introduced allusions to recent events. With their rather loosely connected scenes enacted in mime and interspersed with processions, they would no doubt appear to us less like ballets than great pageants, performed with wonderful precision but lacking in poetry.

The most successful was *Excelsior*, which was given more than a hundred times during 1881, when it was first produced, and was later revived in Paris, London, and St Petersburg. Its theme was the progress of mankind, and the audience was treated to a succession of scenes representing Volta's invention of the electric pile, the invention of the electric telegraph, the building of the Suez Canal, and the piercing of a tunnel through the Alps. *Amor* followed five years later, and was no less than an attempt to cover the history of the human race in a ballet, and finally there was *Sport*, produced in 1897, a grandiose work that foreshadowed the coming century's preoccupation with sport.

The successes of Antonietta dell'Era in Berlin and Irene

Sironi in Vienna were just two more examples of the pre-eminence of Italian ballerinas. In fact, almost the only centre of ballet where they never gained a foothold was Copenhagen. Here, after Bournonville's retirement, the repertory of ballets he had built up was almost reverently preserved through the efforts of Hans Beck. Beck, who was a fine dancer, was responsible for the Danish production of *Coppélia*, in which the emphasis is laid much more on character dancing than in other versions. Italian virtuosity was never introduced into the Royal Danish Ballet at Copenhagen, whose dancers continued to dance like their predecessors in the days of Bournonville. It is fortunate for us that Copenhagen became the backwater that it did during these years, for had it been receptive, like Paris, to every new artistic trend, this precious tradition might have been lost. We should then be unable today to see a style that preserves so much of the lyrical quality of the Romantic period, which, as the nineteenth century drew to its close, tended to be forgotten elsewhere – even, to some extent, in St Petersburg – in the general preoccupation with virtuosity.

CHAPTER SIX

The Age of Petipa

St Petersburg was the capital city of Imperial Russia. Here, for several months in every year, the Tsars lived in their great Winter Palace, which was only one of the city's many splendid buildings. The setting for the ballet *Petrushka* shows us a view of St Petersburg, with the imposing spire of the Admiralty rising into the sky in the background, but the building with which we are most concerned in this chapter is the Maryinsky Theatre, the great opera house which stands in the square that used to be called Theatre Square. The Maryinsky replaced the Bolshoi Theatre as the home of the Imperial Russian Ballet in 1885. Both were state theatres in the widest sense. The Director was appointed personally by the Tsar, and staff, singers, dancers, and musicians were all in a sense Imperial servants, subject to stern discipline but assured of a pension after long and faithful service. This discipline and the seemingly unlimited funds that were expended on the ballet in nineteenth-century Russia were advantages which no other opera house enjoyed in anything like the same measure. Also, in St Petersburg, ballet was given an equal standing with opera, and important ballet productions filled a whole evening's programme. Elsewhere in Europe, what we now call the full-length ballet did not exist. Even if a ballet were divided into two or three acts, such as *Giselle* or *Coppélia*, it was always given with an opera.

The Maryinsky of the late nineteenth century was probably the most glamorous opera house in the world, and this glamour seemed to shine more and more brightly as the rumblings of discontent throughout the country brought the Revolution closer. Most of the seats were reserved for the Court, the diplomatic corps, and members of exclusive clubs, less than a third – and most of those in the gallery and balcony – being available for the public. A considerable proportion of the audience attended nearly every performance. These were the balletomanes, a closely-knit group which gained immense influence in the management of the theatre, imposing their demands not only in details such as the casting of ballets, but even in weightier matters affecting production and policy. They were very conservative in their outlook, and their influence probably retarded the development of the art they enjoyed so much, for it required a strong Director to ignore their demands. Much more progressive were the enthusiasts in the gallery and balcony, students, clerks, and junior officers for the most part, who often queued throughout most of a freezing Russian night to be sure of their seats. Unlike the balletomanes downstairs, they confined their admiration solely to the dancers' performances, and if they did not have the ear of the management, they made their opinions no less felt by the vehemence of their cheers or disapproving whistling. Sometimes they became so unruly that the police had to be sent up to restore order.

We shall be mainly concerned in this chapter with St Petersburg, but Russian ballet, even then, had two centres. Moscow, the other centre, was a merchant city, and the Bolshoi Theatre there could not match the Bolshoi and Maryinsky of St Petersburg either in splendour or in taste. Ballet in Moscow had started in the eighteenth century when an enterprising dancer began training the inmates of the Orphanage. Soon a thriving ballet company was in existence which gave performances that were perhaps more vital, if less polished, than those of St Petersburg, because the Moscow audiences were drawn from a much wider cross-section of the public. As we have seen, at least one great dancer, Sankovskaya, had emerged at the Bolshoi Theatre, and Carlo Blasis spent several years there. As the century wore on, the Moscow ballet more and more developed a character of its own. It often presented works that had already been successfully produced in St Petersburg, but new ballets also figured in its programmes. *Don Quixote* and

Swan Lake both had their first performance in Moscow. However, Moscow was not to assume international importance as a centre of ballet until the twentieth century, when it became the capital of the Soviet Union.

We must now retrace our steps to St Petersburg, where, in 1847, a young Frenchman called Marius Petipa arrived with a contract as *premier danseur*. Today the name of Petipa is well known to everyone who is interested in ballet, for it appears on the programme whenever *Swan Lake* or *The Sleeping Beauty* is presented, but both these ballets were created many years later, towards the end of his career. Unlike many choreographers, Petipa did not become prominent as a young man. He was fifty before he became principal ballet-master in St Petersburg and well over seventy when he staged *The Sleeping Beauty*.

For the first twenty-two years of his stay in Russia, Marius Petipa learnt the craft of the choreographer in the best possible way. He was able to observe at first hand the methods of Jules Perrot and Arthur Saint-Léon, and also – which was no less useful – to learn, from their experience, how to deal with the authorities whose word was felt in the theatre – with the Director and the many officials, and also with the more influential balletomanes. He would have seen how Perrot, brilliant choreographer though he was, lacked the tact and patience to handle these people and so never received proper support, whereas Saint-Léon, who was a lesser artist, was pliable and always ready to adapt himself to meet their wishes. Perrot, after producing expanded versions of many of his great ballets, such as *La Esmeralda*, became frustrated because he was not given enough opportunity to create new ballets, and left Russia in 1859, after which he was to produce no more ballets, although he was then only forty-nine. While Perrot's ballets were distinguished by their dramatic choreography, Saint-Léon's main quality was his ability to tailor a ballet to suit a ballerina – and that was just what the St Petersburg balletomanes were most interested in at that time. He produced one work which has remained constantly popular in

Russia ever since, *The Little Hump-backed Horse*. This ballet was founded on a Russian fairy tale, and although its conventional choreography was by a Frenchman and its music by an Italian, Cesare Pugni, it pointed to the rich material that was to be found in Russian folk-lore.

During these years, Marius Petipa produced several ballets, one of which, *The Daughter of Pharaoh*, was a resounding success, but his main activity at this time was centred on the ballet school. Here he was in charge of the training, and as a result of his efforts Russian ballerinas began to appear who were capable of standing comparison with the visiting foreign stars. Among these were his wife Marie Petipa, Martha Muravieva, and Ekaterina Vazem. Male dancing was not so neglected as it was in the West, but while travesty dancing never obtained a hold as it did in Paris and London, the ballerina was supreme even in Russia. However, St Petersburg possessed several fine male dancers, including Pavel Gerdt, one of the greatest *danseurs nobles* of all time, and the fiery character dancer, Felix Kshesinsky.

When Marius Petipa at last succeeded to the post of principal ballet-master in 1869, ballet in Russia had reached a low ebb, having lost much of the popularity it had enjoyed in Romantic times. Petipa at first showed no unusual originality, and for a dozen years filled his ballets with bravura *variations* and eye-catching scenic effects, and neglected the male dancers, much as Saint-Léon had done before him. When Bournonville visited St Petersburg in the seventies, he was shocked to find that dramatic effect had been sacrificed in the interests of virtuosity and vulgarity. He did not conceal his concern, but Petipa and his colleague Christian Johansson explained that they had no alternative but to give the public what it wanted and comply with the demands of the management. Two of Petipa's ballets from this period have survived: *Don Quixote*, first produced in Moscow in 1869 and still performed in its entirety in Russia, though in a later version by Gorsky, and known in the West chiefly on account of its *grand pas de deux*, which many ballerinas use as a show-piece of technical fireworks; and *The Bayadere*, which dates from 1877.

The rage for ballet which we associate with the Russia of the Tsars did not begin until the eighteen-eighties. It was largely brought about by the intelligent and cultured Director of the Imperial Theatres, Vsevolojsky, who took a very active interest in the ballet. Petipa, who accepted his authority with good grace, then entered upon the most glorious phase of his career. Ballet became fashionable again in St Petersburg quite suddenly with the triumphant appearance in 1885 of Virginia Zucchi, the first of a line of Italian ballerinas to visit Russia, but its popularity was finally sealed with the production of *The Sleeping Beauty* in 1890. This ballet marked the summit of Vsevolojsky's achievement. He had instituted a fundamental reform in suppressing the post of official composer of ballet music, which Pugni and Minkus had held, and instead of facile and tuneful scores of no musical importance the audiences of the Maryinsky now heard the rich melodies of Tchaikovsky.

Tchaikovsky had already composed one ballet, *Swan Lake*, but this had been so wretchedly produced in Moscow in 1877 that he became almost convinced that ballet was not his field. He called his score 'poor stuff' in comparison with Delibes' *Sylvia*, and did not turn his thoughts to ballet again until Vsevolojsky commissioned him to compose *The Sleeping Beauty* twelve years later. Petipa, who had worked out the complete scheme of the ballet in advance, presented him with detailed instructions for the tempo and length of each passage, but this did not appear to hamper him, for he produced a score that sparkled with fresh melodies and rich orchestral effects. The ballet was a triumph for both the composer and the choreographer when given its first performance at the Maryinsky in 1890, even though the Tsar, Nicholas II, could think of nothing better to say than a banal 'Very nice' when Tchaikovsky was presented. The composer was very hurt, and rightly so, for the ballet has remained a classic in Russia and has never left the repertory of the theatre in which it was created. It was also to be revived by Diaghilev in London with great splendour, and later still to become the most popular classic in the repertory of Britain's Royal Ballet.

The leading role of the Princess Aurora was danced, not by a Russian dancer, but by the Milanese ballerina, Carlotta Brianza. This was the result of the influx of Italian stars which had been one of the features of Russian ballet in the eighteen-eighties. It had started in a summer theatre in the Livadia amusement park, where Virginia Zucchi had made her first St Petersburg appearance in a faery extravaganza. In no time everyone was talking of the 'divine Virginia', who opened up new possibilities by her forceful dramatic dancing and her radiant femininity. Her engagement at the Maryinsky, where she enjoyed a fantastic triumph, was largely due to the critic Skalkovsky, who wrote that there was more poetry in her back than in all the modern Italian poets put together. To many, she proved that a dancer could be as great an artist as Sarah Bernhardt or Duse. Alexandre Benois, who was to become one of Diaghilev's principal collaborators, was carried away with enthusiasm, as were so many others that ballet regained its fashionable appeal almost overnight.

Zucchi was a dancer-actress rather than a virtuoso, but the Italian ballerinas who followed her owed their success principally to their technical accomplishments, particularly in turning and *pointe* work. Petipa did not favour the engagement of these Italian ballerinas, because they were not his own pupils. He always preferred working with Russian dancers: with Vazem, a cold but brilliant technician for whom he created *The Bayadere*, with the graceful Evgenia Sokolova, with Varvara Nikitina for whom he staged the first Russian production of *Coppélia* in 1884, or with his daughter who was named Marie after her mother. But none the less he not only accepted the Italian guests but cheerfully created important roles for them.

This Italian invasion was not confined to ballerinas. It also brought to Russia a male dancer, Enrico Cecchetti, whose first experience of a Russian public, like Zucchi's, was in a popular theatre, where he produced and danced in a version of *Excel-*

sior in 1887. He too was soon engaged by Vsevolojsky, and was given two roles to create in *The Sleeping Beauty*: the wicked fairy Carabosse, which brought out his great talent as a mime, and the Blue Bird, which displayed his equally brilliant gifts as a dancer. To the Russian audiences he was the male counterpart of Zucchi. They were amazed by his virtuosity. His wonderfully intricate *entrechats* and pirouettes surpassed anything which Russian dancers could perform. By his example, Cecchetti did much to restore the popularity and prestige of the male dancer in Russia.

Tchaikovsky followed up *The Sleeping Beauty* with *The Nutcracker*, which was produced in 1892. Petipa had planned this ballet with his usual thoroughness, but he was taken ill during its preparation and the task of arranging the choreography devolved on his assistant, Lev Ivanov. In the brilliant *divertissement* at the end, the part of the Sugar Plum Fairy was danced at the first performance by the Italian ballerina, Antonietta dell'Era, but at the second performance the role was taken over by a Russian dancer, Varvara Nikitina.

Lev Ivanov was to cooperate in the production of the third Tchaikovsky ballet to be produced at the Maryinsky, *Swan Lake*. As we have already seen, this had been a failure in Moscow, but Marius Petipa was at a loss to understand how this could have happened unless the production and the choreography had been at fault. So he sent to Moscow for the score, and had little difficulty in persuading Vsevolojsky to agree to its being revived, in a revised form, at the Maryinsky. Tchaikovsky had recently died of cholera, and it was Drigo, the conductor, who put the necessary final touches to the score. He orchestrated some of Tchaikovsky's piano pieces to fill out the last act, and composed the music for the Prince's *variation* in the ballroom scene. As usual, Petipa worked out the scheme for the production, but he only arranged the choreography of the first and third acts. The second and fourth acts – the lake-side scenes which are filled mainly with the dances for the swans – were left to Ivanov, whose inspired choreography captured the lyrical quality of Tchaikovsky's music to form a wonderful dance poem which has lost none of its emotional impact over the years.

The second act of *Swan Lake* was ready first, and this was first performed on its own at a memorial performance for Tchaikovsky in 1894. The complete ballet was not given until early the following year. Another Italian virtuoso, Pierina Legnani, was given the honour of creating the famous dual role of Odette and Odile – the princess who has been turned into a swan, and the evil magician's daughter who assumes her form – and her great feat of performing thirty-two consecutive *fouettés*, which no one had done in St Petersburg before her, is still preserved in present-day Russian and British productions of the ballet.

After the death of Tchaikovsky, Petipa had to work with lesser composers. Only one of these could claim distinction as a musician in his own right, and that was Glazounov, a difficult and obstinate man who would not alter his music to suit Petipa's requirements. His most famous ballet score was *Raymonda*, which is still given in Russia, but his music is also heard at Covent Garden when the Royal Ballet dance Ashton's *Birthday Offering*. Another melodious score composed at the turn of the century was Drigo's *Harlequin's Millions*.

It is astonishing to realize that Marius Petipa was a man of seventy-five when *Swan Lake* was first produced in St Petersburg and that even then he had not exhausted his creative activity. Now, in the last years of his long career, he found himself able to work with Russian ballerinas again, for a brilliant new generation was emerging. Much of the credit for this was due to Christian Johansson, a pupil of Bournonville, who, after dancing at the Maryinsky for nearly thirty years, had become the chief teacher in 1869. He, more than anyone else, fashioned what we know today as the Russian school of dancing but which he always insisted was the French school which the French themselves had forgotten.

The Italian brilliance of execution was soon assimilated into the Russian style, and by the turn of the century visiting Italian ballerinas no longer had anything new to offer. Mathilda

Kshesinska, for instance, could match all their feats: she was the first Russian ballerina to perform the thirty-two *fouettés*, and she was given the title of *prima ballerina assoluta*, which only Legnani had held before her. Her contemporary, Olga Preobrajenska, did not rise to fame so quickly, but she was no less great in her own way, being a delightful comedienne. A wealth of other dancers followed – Vera Trefilova, Lubov Egorova, Julia Sedova, Anna Pavlova – all of whom graduated from the Maryinsky ballet school in the nineties, while at the same time, male dancing was coming into its own again with the appearance of Nicolas and Serge Legat, Alexander Gorsky, Georgi Kyaksht, and Michel Fokine.

While this brilliant new generation of Russian dancers was emerging, a group of progressive young artists and art-lovers under the growing influence of Serge Diaghilev were airing their views in a magazine called *The World of Art*. Prince Volkonsky was a friend of this group, and when he succeeded Vsevolojsky as Director of the Imperial Theatres, he called in Diaghilev to take complete charge of a new production of *Sylvia*. Unfortunately he regretted this bold act within a few days, but when he asked Diaghilev to relinquish some of his authority so as not to cause too much offence to the officials of the theatre, Diaghilev flatly refused. Volkonsky pleaded with Diaghilev to be reasonable, but events were already beyond his control and soon afterwards the Tsar signed Diaghilev's summary dismissal.

Volkonsky's turn was not long in coming. His reforming zeal was disapproved of in many influential circles, and he was eventually placed in a situation where he had no alternative but to resign. He had given instructions that Kshesinka was to wear panniers in a ballet which was set in the eighteenth century. The ballerina refused, and was duly fined by Volkonsky for disobedience. The Tsar then intervened by having it conveyed to Volkonsky that he wanted the fine publicly cancelled. Volkonsky had no choice in the matter, but after he had complied with the Tsar's wishes he sent in his resignation.

Volkonsky was succeeded by Teliakovsky, a professional

soldier who set about the task of introducing reforms with little regard for the feelings of Marius Petipa, who was well over eighty years of age. Petipa's last ballet for the Maryinsky was *The Magic Mirror*, which was produced in 1903. He did not like Koreshchenko's music from the start, but was even unhappier about the sets and costumes, which were designed by Golovine, an artist of the modern school. Teliakovsky refused to withdraw the ballet, and when it proved a failure, Petipa was convinced that he was the victim of a plot. The jeering laughter that greeted the ballet haunted the old man to the end of his days. It was revived just once for the *corps de ballet*'s benefit gala, which had been planned to close with a little ceremony when the company were to present Petipa with a silver laurel wreath in the presence of the public. But the management refused to allow the curtain to be raised again at the end, and Vera Trefilova had to make the presentation almost surreptitiously in the wings. Petipa went into retirement, thinking he had been a failure. The management's pettiness was carried to the point of refusing him admittance to the stage of the Maryinsky, a ban that wounded him cruelly.

The turn in Petipa's fortunes was more than a rebellion of the younger generation against the authority he had wielded for so long. New ideas were beginning to emerge that were to influence the future course of ballet. The whole conception of the art, it was felt, needed to be revised. The most important factor in a ballet should be the idea behind it, to which everything else must be subordinated to give it the maximum force and meaning. At the same time, an improvement was called for in the music. Good music was still the exception at the Maryinsky, but the American dancer, Isadora Duncan, was to show how a fine score could add to the emotional impact of the dance when she visited St Petersburg in 1905. Meanwhile, *The World of Art* was campaigning for a more positive approach in the design of scenery and costumes. There was also a choreographer's problem. This was to restore warmth and feeling to the dance, and to assimilate the recent innovations in technique by using them as means of expression rather than as sheer feats of virtuosity. The fulfilment of these ideas was to bring about the great revival of ballet which we associate with the names of Fokine and Diaghilev.

CHAPTER SEVEN

Diaghilev

SERGE DIAGHILEV was one of those great men who from time to time appear in our midst and shape events. In the history of ballet outside Russia we talk of the years from 1909 to 1929 as the Diaghilev period, much as people speak of the Napoleonic age in the wider field of world history. Although he was neither a choreographer nor a dancer himself, he accomplished nothing less than a complete revival of ballet. With a strength of purpose that was almost superhuman, and the gift of guiding dancers, choreographers, musicians, and designers to work together towards the end which he himself had conceived, he raised ballet from a diverting entertainment to a serious theatrical art which absorbed the creative energies of the greatest artists and musicians of his time. He gave it a loftier purpose than it had ever had before, and he shaped its whole future course everywhere save, ironically, in his native Russia.

The story of the Diaghilev Ballet is inseparably bound up with the character of its founder, and we cannot appreciate the company without understanding the man. Diaghilev was born and brought up many hundreds of miles east of St Petersburg, in the very heart of Russia, and though he spent so many of his mature years in Western Europe, he always remained essentially Russian. So too did his company, despite the collaboration of dancers, artists, musicians, and poets of other nationalities. The Diaghilev Ballet was a unique organization, which to Western eyes appeared glamorous, exotic, and excitingly bohemian. In a sort of way it resembled the serf companies which in days gone by had been formed by many wealthy Russian landowners, for Diaghilev was and remained to the end its sole master. So absolute was his authority that his dancers always felt they were dancing primarily for him, and his approval mattered more to them than anything else.

When Diaghilev presented a ballet, it was because it fitted in with his ideas, and not because it was what the public wanted. As the story of his company unfolds, we shall see how the problems which had arisen by the turn of the century were solved, and how the art of ballet was brought into a most intimate alliance with music and painting – no longer the tuneful accompaniments and the realistic scenery which were all too often the rule in the nineteenth century, but all that was finest and most progressive in these two arts. This was the great achievement of the Diaghilev Ballet.

Music played an important part in Diaghilev's life from his earliest days, for his family, who were well-to-do country gentry, were absorbed by such a passion for music that if they had nothing to do, they were quite capable of passing the time by improvising a performance of an opera. There was never a thought, however, that he might embark on a musical, let alone a theatrical, career, and he was sent to St Petersburg to study law at the university. There, by a happy chance, he fell in with a group of remarkably brilliant young artists and intellectuals who were united in a common quest for knowledge and truth. At first, his new companions thought him provincial and gauche, but he soon impressed them with his vital and exuberant personality and his astonishing grasp of any subject which he cared to take up.

The leader of this group was a young art student called Alexandre Benois, among whose many enthusiasms was an ardent love of the ballet. His youthful passion for Virginia Zucchi had so carried him away that one evening he had waited for her outside the Maryinsky stage-door and laid his coat on the pavement for her to step on as she walked to her carriage. Another prominent member who was to play an important part in Diaghilev's life was Léon Bakst, a young artist of Jewish origin, whose early efforts gave little idea of the sensational mastery of colour that was to make him famous.

When Diaghilev joined them, the interests of these young

men ranged over many subjects, but in time their aims crystal-ized into the single purpose of bringing about an artistic revi-val in Russia. By then, Diaghilev, whom they had not taken very seriously at first, had become their leader, and it was due to his drive that the magazine, *The World of Art*, was founded in 1898 with himself as editor. During the six years of its existence this magazine exerted great influence by opposing the sterile academism into which Russian art had fallen, and by strengthening the links between Russian and European art. The task of editing it did not absorb all Diaghilev's time and energy, however, for at the same time he was adding to his reputation by organizing a series of exhibitions that culminated in a fabulous display of historical portraits, for which he had searched the length and breadth of Russia.

Despite his great love and knowledge of music, Diaghilev was not immediately attracted to the ballet. His first visit, when he saw *The Sleeping Beauty*, did not make any special im-pression on him, and it was not until he saw *Raymonda* a num-ber of years later that he began to take a real interest. This was very shortly before his association with the Maryinsky which was brought to such an abrupt end after his difference with Volkonsky over the proposed production of *Sylvia*.

Although as a result he was excluded from the Maryinsky, he was still able to keep in touch with events there through Benois and Bakst, both of whom soon began working ser-iously for the stage. Bakst designed his first ballet for the Maryinsky, *The Fairy Doll*, in 1903, and four years later Benois entered the field with *The Pavilion of Armida*, for which he not only designed the scenery and costumes but wrote the scenario as well. This was an important work, and was produced by a young choreographer of the most remarkable promise, Michel Fokine, who had come to Diaghilev for advice two years before, when he was implicated in a movement to reform the ballet.

Some of the younger dancers, headed by Fokine, Pavlova, and Karsavina, had wanted to have a greater say in artistic matters and the conditions of their employment, and when disturbances broke out in St Petersburg in the autumn of 1905, they saw an opportunity of pressing their demands. Their little revolt failed, as did the revolution that threatened on the streets, and although none of them was victimized, they returned to their duties with heavy hearts. For they had learnt that Serge Legat, one of the most brilliant of their number, had cut his throat – out of shame, some said, at having let his comrades down by signing a declaration of loyalty to the management.

For Fokine, the failure of the dancers' revolt was of little importance compared with the benefits he was to gain from associating with *The World of Art* circle. At the Imperial Ballet School he had been such an outstanding pupil that he was given important parts from the moment of his début without being made to pass through the *corps de ballet*, and he became a teacher himself at the age of twenty-two. His interests were far from being limited to ballet. He had a wide cultural background, was a talented painter, and had studied at the drama school. He was also a man of great intelligence who thought for himself and was not content with slavishly following in the footsteps of his predecessors. Even as a young man he realized that the art of ballet had possibilities which no one had yet explored. He saw how choreographers were prevented from realizing their ideas fully because of meaningless traditions. Mime, for example, had degenerated into a sort of sign language, ballerinas' costumes were invariably based on the same style of tutu, the recent progress in technique had resulted in dancers neglecting the upper part of their bodies, and – most hampering of all to the choreographer – everything was subordinated to the demands of the prima ballerina, who had to be shown to best effect. Fokine wanted to concentrate everything, even the role of the prima ballerina, on making the ballet as a whole as effective as possible, and in particular he wanted his dancers to move with expression flowing through their whole bodies. He began working out these ideas in his earliest ballets, and was so successful that old Petipa prophesied that he had a great future before him.

Meanwhile, Diaghilev was spending much of his time in Paris, promoting Russian art. The political climate was very favourable for such an enterprise, for the Franco-Russian alliance had just been signed. He began with an exhibition of Russian art, and followed this with a series of concerts at the Opéra in which many great figures in Russian music took part, including Chaliapine, whose bass voice held Paris enthralled for the first time. The next year Diaghilev presented a season of Russian opera, and when this was over, he returned to Russia with a new project forming in his mind for the summer of 1909: a season of Russian opera and ballet.

Diaghilev now commanded great prestige in St Petersburg, and with the support of the Grand Duke Vladimir, his plans took shape rapidly in the early months of 1909. Fokine was engaged as ballet-master, and Diaghilev had every hope of taking with him to Paris the best dancers from St Petersburg and Moscow. Unluckily, the Grand Duke died suddenly almost at the last moment, and deprived of his patron, Diaghilev found himself faced with many difficulties. The Tsar withdrew his offer of a subsidy, and Kshesinska and Gerdt changed their minds about going. Undismayed, Diaghilev reduced his operatic programme, and with French backing, arranged to give a season, not at the Paris Opéra, but at the Châtelet Theatre.

The great Russian critic, Svetlov, who accompanied the company to Paris, wrote of this first season of the Diaghilev Ballet that it should be commemorated in the annals of Russian ballet in letters of gold. Paris was bathed in spring sunshine when the company arrived, but there was little time to enjoy the beauties of the city, for soon everyone was hard at work rehearsing and preparing for the opening. Much had to be done in a short time. It was necessary to re-lay the stage, and Diaghilev ordered the auditorium to be redecorated, regardless of expense.

The first public performance of the Diaghilev Ballet on 19 May 1909, was a glittering occasion. Paris society was present in force, and Diaghilev, with his unfailing flair for publicity placed all the most beautiful actresses of the day together in the

1. Margot Fonteyn and Michael Somes in *Ondine* (*Houston Rogers*)

2a. *Balet Comique de la Royne.* Performed before Henri III of France and Catherine de' Medici in 1581

2b. Louis XIV as Apollo in the court ballet, *Les Nopces de Pélée et de Thétis*, performed in 1654 (*Bibliothèque de l'Institut, Paris*)

3. Marie Anne de Camargo. Oil painting by Nicolas Lancret

4a. Jean-Georges Noverre. Pastel portrait by J. B. Perronneau, 1764 (*Musée de l'Opéra, Paris*)

4b. A scene from Noverre's *Medea and Jason* as performed in London in 1781, with (*left to right*) Giovanna Baccelli, Gaëtan Vestris, and Mme Simonet

5a. Marie Taglioni and her brother Paul in *La Sylphide*. Oil painting by G. Lepaulle, 1834 (*Musée des Arts Décoratifs, Paris*)

5b. Auguste Vestris. Engraving by Bartolozzi and Pastorini from an aquatint attributed to John Dance

6a. Carlotta Grisi and Lucien Petipa in *Giselle*. Lithograph from a drawing by Victor Coindre

6b. Virginia Zucchi in *La Esmeralda*

7a. Vaslav Nijinsky in *Le Spectre de la Rose* (*Raymond Mander and Joe Mitchenson Theatre Collection*)

7b. Tamara Karsavina in *The Firebird*. Oil painting by J. E. Blanche (*Collection of Serge Lifar*)

8. Leonide Massine in *The Three-Cornered Hat* (Collection of Peter Revitt)

9. Olga Spessivtseva in *The Sleeping Princess*

10. Anton Dolin and Lydia Sokolova in *The Blue Train*

11. Anna Pavlova in *The Dying Swan* (*Nicholas Yarovoff*)

12a. Tatiana Riabouchinska in *Les Présages* (*Anthony*)

12b. Tamara Toumanova in *Symphonie Fantastique* (*Anthony*)

circle. But this première was much more than a social occasion, it was a major landmark in the history of the theatre. Ballet staked its claim to be a major theatrical art that evening, when the company's extraordinary triumph made it a main topic of conversation not only in high society but, what was much more important, among artists and intellectuals.

Never within living memory had Paris seen a male dancer to compare with Vaslav Nijinsky, who created a sensation with his soaring elevation and astonishing lightness and his mysterious Slavonic allure. His triumph overshadowed the personal successes of all the rest of the company, Anna Pavlova and Tamara Karsavina included. Pavlova, who had come with the greatest reputation of all, was said to have been offended by the Parisians' predilection for Nijinsky, and danced for Diaghilev only once more after this first season. Her story belongs to another chapter, but Karsavina was to remain with Diaghilev and share many of Nijinsky's triumphs. With her expressive features and large, deep brown eyes, she was the ideal interpreter of Fokine's ballets, for she danced with her whole body, giving expression to every movement.

The repertory which Diaghilev had brought to Paris included four ballets, all by Fokine, and a *divertissement*. Of the ballets, it was the two exotic works which created the greatest impression. The Polovtsian Dances from Borodin's opera *Prince Igor*, with their wild rhythms and Adolph Bolm dominating the stage with tremendous virility as the Polovtsian Chief, had a shattering effect on the unsuspecting and refined Paris audience. The other exotic ballet, *Cleopatra*, has not survived. It was inspired by a ballet in the Maryinsky repertory, but Diaghilev had changed the music and presented it with vivid scenery and costumes by Bakst. Pavlova and Karsavina both played important roles, but the central figure of Cleopatra was taken by a superbly beautiful young Jewess who had been a private pupil of Fokine – Ida Rubinstein.

The other two ballets were *The Pavilion of Armida* and *Les Sylphides*. Apart from introducing Nijinsky, the first made little impression, and even the haunting beauty of *Les Sylphides*, with Pavlova, Karsavina, and Nijinsky, was somewhat over-shadowed by the powerful impact of *Prince Igor* and *Cleopatra*. Time was to prove what a perfect ballet *Les Sylphides* was, and still is, for it is now probably the most frequently performed ballet in the whole of the modern repertory. Except for the overture, which Diaghilev himself suggested, and Benois' new scenery, it was a revival of a ballet which Fokine had arranged to a selection of music by Chopin for a pupils' performance in St Petersburg under the title of *Chopiniana*. It was Diaghilev, too, who decided that the title should be changed to *Les Sylphides*. Although it had no plot, the ballet conjured up those ethereal spirits that haunted the stage in the days of the Roman-tic Ballet, and the new title conveyed the work's meaning to perfection with its suggestion of the legendary Taglioni's greatest role.

After such a resounding success, a return visit in 1910 was a foregone conclusion. This time Diaghilev was approached by the Paris Opéra to give his season there, and he set to work preparing for it, realizing that everything depended on his recapturing the same excitement he had aroused the previous year. Pavlova and Bolm could not join him, but he still had Karsavina and Nijinsky, and in addition he engaged two dancers from Moscow, Alexander Volinine and Ekaterina Geltzer. As for the repertory, Benois had persuaded him to include a revival of *Giselle*, and he also planned to present three new works by Fokine, each of which has stood the test of time: *The Firebird*, *Le Carnaval*, and *Scheherazade*.

The previous year's triumph was more than equalled in 1910, it was surpassed, despite the rather lukewarm reception of *Giselle*, which the French found old-fashioned and musically thin. Again it was the exotic works which appealed most. *Scheherazade* was based on an idea by Benois, but to his disgust, the credit on the programme was given to Bakst, whose gorgeously colourful scenery and costumes had a strong in-fluence both on fashion and interior decoration. Fokine's choreography, inspired by a study of Persian miniatures, was so effective that it seemed that Rimsky-Korsakov's music had been specially written for it, rather than the choreography being based on existing music. Ida Rubinstein played the role of Zobeida, the Shah's favourite wife, who, when her lord and master is away, makes love to a slave, and Nijinsky created yet another sensation with his feline interpretation of the Golden Slave.

Le Carnaval was a lighter work which Fokine had produced before for a charity performance in St Petersburg. It was a delicate evocation of the Italian *commedia dell'arte* with a German flavour that was conveyed in Schumann's music and Bakst's costumes, and Nijinsky and Karsavina played the parts of Harlequin and Columbine with a subtle, almost satirical humour.

But by far the most important work of this season was *The Firebird*, a ballet based on Russian folk-lore, which, thanks to its brilliant score, had an atmosphere of mysterious fantasy. It was a musical event of the first importance, for it introduced to the field of ballet a brilliant young composer, Igor Stravinsky, a discovery of Diaghilev. Diaghilev's judgement was triumphantly confirmed, for Stravinsky was to become the greatest ballet composer of his time. His scores marked a great stride forward in the development of ballet music, so much so in fact that when the dancers began rehearsing *The Firebird*, they found his rhythms strange and difficult. Pavlova, who was originally to have taken the title-role, disliked the music so much that she refused to dance to it, and the part was created by Karsavina instead, with Fokine himself playing the Tsarevitch. The composer worked in very close collaboration with Fokine, and the ballet can truly be said to have been a joint work. The original scenery and costumes were by Golovine, Goncharova's décor which is used in today's Royal Ballet production being designed when Diaghilev re-staged the ballet in 1926.

Diaghilev's triumph at the Opéra was so great that he was pressed to give three additional performances. Karsavina had a long-standing engagement in London, and it was necessary to give *The Firebird* without her. To replace her, Diaghilev chose a very young dancer called Lydia Lopokova, who was so enchanting that an American impresario lured her away and she was lost to the company for several years.

For its first two seasons, the Diaghilev Ballet was a scratch company collected together only for the summer months and then disbanded. Now, however, Diaghilev decided to form a permanent company with Fokine as his ballet-master, and Nijinsky and Karsavina as the principal dancers. By a fortunate circumstance, Nijinsky was forced to resign from the Maryinsky at about this time after a scandal caused by his wearing a costume in *Giselle* that was not approved of, and as a result he was free to become a permanent member of Diaghilev's company. Fokine and Karsavina also accepted Diaghilev's proposals, while maintaining their connexion with the Maryinsky, and Enrico Cecchetti, probably the greatest living teacher of classical ballet, agreed to join him as a teacher. The company was to be centred on Monte Carlo, and thenceforward the dancers were to acknowledge Diaghilev as their sole master. This they did gladly, for though discipline was sternly enforced, Diaghilev was always to care for them and pay them well, taking little for his own needs. The first year of the permanent company's existence, 1911, augured well for the future, for it saw the creation of two immortal ballets by Fokine, *Le Spectre de la Rose* and *Petrushka*, and a very successful first London season.

The idea for *Le Spectre de la Rose* was suggested by the French poet Vaudoyer and was taken from a poem by Gautier. To the music of Weber's 'Invitation to the Dance', it conjured up the romantic dream of a young girl who has just returned home from her first ball. Karsavina played the young girl with exquisite delicacy, but it was above all a triumph for Nijinsky as the Spirit of the Rose. His final leap through the open window has become a legend. Somehow he contrived it so that it seemed to the audience that he was soaring into the air as he disappeared from view. In reality, he landed in the wings, so utterly exhausted that Diaghilev's manservant had to be waiting to revive him with a cup of black coffee and a towel before he could make his way to his dressing-room.

Petrushka is the greatest of all the masterpieces that Diaghilev presented. It is such a perfect example of collaboration between choreographer, musician, and designer that it is impossible to rate any one above the others. The origin of the ballet can be traced to a burlesque concerto which Stravinsky wrote in the form of a duel between a puppet, represented by the piano, and the orchestra. Diaghilev was so taken with this piece when he first heard it that he at once wanted to make a ballet out of it, and in his inimitable way, he soon had Stravinsky, Benois, and Fokine working on the idea. It had long been Benois' dream to recreate St Petersburg's Butter Week Fair in a ballet, and he not only worked out the details of the scenario but designed the scenery and costumes. Stravinsky expanded his concerto, and his score conveyed to perfection the bustling atmosphere of the fairground, which Fokine for his part reproduced so brilliantly in his choreography. Petrushka, the pathetic, ill-used sawdust puppet who has a soul over which his master, the Charlatan, has no control, was considered to be Nijinsky's greatest role, although it gave him no opportunity of displaying his wonderful technical gifts as a dancer.

Until now Diaghilev's repertory had been entirely produced by Fokine, who was only in his early thirties and still at the height of his creative activity. Diaghilev, however, was burning to strike out in new directions, and he did not feel that Fokine, whose ideas and style were fully formed, was the man for his experiments. Surreptitiously, therefore, he began preparing Nijinsky to be a choreographer. When Fokine discovered what was happening he was deeply offended and resigned from the company, without so much as a protest from Diaghilev. Before Fokine left, however, he presented Diaghilev with proof of his undimmed talent by producing three new ballets *The Blue God, Thamar*, a ballet with a Caucasian theme which remained a popular work in the Diaghilev repertory for many years, and finally *Daphnis and Chloe*. Ravel had been working on the score for this ballet for about two years, and the subject was one which had long appealed to Fokine. The ballet was given with scenery and costumes by Bakst, and was a deserved success when first performed with Nijinsky and Karsavina at the Paris Opéra in the summer of 1912.

By then Nijinsky's first ballet had already been given, and had given the Diaghilev Ballet its first 'scandal'. Nijinsky was both a superb dancer and, as he had shown in *Petrushka*, an instinctive actor who became transformed the moment he stepped before the footlights, but off-stage he gave the impression of being only moderately intelligent, for he could not express himself in any other way than in his dancing. Somehow Diaghilev wanted to mould Nijinsky's mind, which he felt was capable of creating great works. Soon he was devoting much time to giving the young dancer an artistic education, with the object of launching him as a choreographer. For the subject of Nijinsky's first ballet, he had chosen Debussy's *L'Après-midi d'un Faune*, and behind closed doors the two of them began to prepare it in the manner of an ancient Greek bas-relief with strange rhythmic movements, performed as in two dimensions, that bore little relation to classic ballet technique. But it was not the unusual structure of the choreography which shocked half the Paris audience into loud protest on the first night, but the final pose when Nijinsky, as the faun, pressed the nymph's scarf to his body. Diaghilev answered the uproar that broke out at the end by ordering the ballet to be repeated, but at later performances the offending pose was modified.

This short ten-minute ballet had required over a hundred rehearsals. Choreography came to Nijinsky with painful difficulty, but Diaghilev made him persevere with two more new ballets which were presented during the company's Paris season of 1913. The lesser of the two was *Jeux*, also to music by Debussy, a curious work danced in tennis costume that suggested the emotions of adolescence, but its reception was nothing compared with that of Nijinsky's next ballet, *The Rite of Spring*. This ballet aimed at evoking primitive pagan ritual on the plains of Russia, and Stravinsky had composed a score that marvellously suggested vast primeval forces but was far from being obviously danceable. The company disliked the ballet, which again had no relationship with classical technique. An enormous number of rehearsals were necessary, and Stravinsky's patience was sorely tried by Nijinsky's apparent ignorance of basic musical principles. Finally, to help Nijinsky with the choreography, Diaghilev had to engage Marie Rambert, a pupil of Jaques Dalcroze, the inventor of a system of rhythmical movement called Dalcroze Eurhythmics. At last the ballet opened. The uproar that broke out in the theatre from the opening bars of the music and continued throughout the first performance made the reception of *L'Après-midi d'un Faune* seem polite by comparison. Spectators actually came to blows in the theatre, and Diaghilev had to stand up in his box and beg the audience to allow the dancers to finish the ballet.

Later that same year the company sailed to South America, while Diaghilev, who had a great fear of the sea, remained behind in Europe. During the voyage, Nijinsky became engaged to a young Hungarian dancer who had recently joined the company, and within a few days of reaching Buenos Aires the couple were married. Diaghilev received the news as a betrayal, for he realized that he could no longer hope to exercise his influence over Nijinsky, whom he curtly and ruthlessly dismissed from the company.

Far from being overwhelmed by the loss of his most sensational dancer and his new ballet-master, Diaghilev decided to re-engage Fokine. This was no easy task, for Fokine had left the company with bitter feelings, but Diaghilev talked him round in a single telephone conversation that lasted for no less than five hours.

The principal project for 1914 was *The Legend of Joseph*, for which Diaghilev had engaged a young dancer whom he had found in Moscow on the point of abandoning ballet to become an actor. His name was Leonide Massine, and the ballet is remembered today not because of its specially written score by Richard Strauss, but because it was the ballet in which Massine played his first important role. The season's highlight, however, proved to be Fokine's production of Rimsky-Korsakov's opera *Le Coq d'Or*, brilliantly designed by Goncharova, with the singers ranged at the sides of the stage and the theme enacted by dancers, including Karsavina as the Queen of Shemakhan and Cecchetti as the Astrologer.

Diaghilev's London season closed only a few days before the outbreak of the First World War, which not only shattered the company's future plans but marked the close of the first and most brilliant period in its existence. More ballets have survived from this period, from 1909 to 1914, than from all the fifteen years that followed. It is in fact the critical period during which our modern conception of ballet took shape, the conception that ballet is a composite art made up of three elements – choreography, music, and décor – which should all be equally balanced. Also, the one-act ballet became the rule not only because it made for a greater variety in the arrangement of an evening's programme, but also because it was the ideal form for the new type of ballet which had taken the place of the lengthy multi-act works of the Petipa period.

In these five years Fokine had rediscovered some of the basic principles of choreography that had long been forgotten, and during his last season with Diaghilev, in 1914, he wrote an important letter to *The Times* in which he set them out. The underlying idea behind his Five Rules was that everything should be directed towards making a ballet as expressive as possible. First, the choreography must not be a mere combination of established dance steps, but an original creation of movement that corresponds with the subject, the period, and the setting of the ballet. Secondly, dancing and mime must be used solely to further the dramatic action. Thirdly, conventional gesture is admissible only where the style of the ballet requires it, and otherwise the dancers must be expressive through their whole bodies. Fourthly, groups and ensembles must be arranged with the purpose of adding expression to the ballet, and not for mere ornament. Lastly, ballet is an alliance of the arts, and the composer and the designer must be given complete liberty to create.

It was not easy to obtain engagements in wartime, but eventually Diaghilev negotiated an American visit for his company in 1916. He, Bakst, Stravinsky, Massine, and the futurist artist Larionov were in Lausanne, but most of the dancers had dispersed and the company had to be built up afresh. Fokine had returned to Russia and did not wish to leave in wartime, and Karsavina, who was in St Petersburg expecting a baby, was also unavailable. The American impresario, however, had made one stipulation: Nijinsky must be included in the company. This presented a very great difficulty, since Nijinsky had been interned in Hungary at the outbreak of war, but Diaghilev went to great lengths to obtain his release. When Nijinsky arrived in New York, the other dancers were all struck by his vague and unfriendly attitude. His mind seemed to be poisoned against Diaghilev, and when a second engagement was arranged for the company with the same stipulation that he should be included, Nijinsky insisted on Diaghilev giving him complete control. Diaghilev bowed to this demand in the interests of the company, and sailed back to Europe with Massine to prepare new ballets. In his absence, however, complete chaos reigned, and the company's reputation in the United States was so severely damaged that it was never able to return there.

Diaghilev's thoughts were now turning more and more towards the future. He was convinced that Fokine had no more to offer him, and he realized Nijinsky's shortcomings as a choreographer. His search for someone to interpret the fruits of his imagination now rested on Massine, whose mind he was delighted to discover was brilliantly alert and receptive. Under the guidance of Diaghilev and Larionov, Massine absorbed a broad artistic education, and when he arrived in Rome with Diaghilev, he began preparing his first important ballet, *The Good-humoured Ladies*, which the company presented on their return from America in 1917. It was based on an eighteenth-century Italian comedy and had music of the same period chosen from the works of Scarlatti. Bakst designed the scenery and costumes, and Lydia Lopokova, who had rejoined the company in America, Lubov Tchernicheva, old Cecchetti and his wife, Massine, and two remarkable Polish male dancers, Stanislas Idzikowski and Leon Woizikovski, took the leading roles. It was a delightful ballet, which had been rehearsed with such thoroughness that its production was well nigh perfect.

The Russian Revolution of 1917 severed Diaghilev's links with Russia, and from then on he was to turn more and more to artists and musicians of Western Europe for new ideas. In the summer of that year, when the war was passing through its most terrible stage, he gave a season in Paris and showed his sympathy with the advanced School of Paris by presenting a new ballet by Massine called *Parade*. This was a very modern ballet, with a scenario by Jean Cocteau, who had been a friend of Diaghilev since his first Paris season. 'Astonish me, Jean,' Diaghilev used to say to him, and this was one of the results.

To the artistic and intellectual world of Paris, ballet was like a new toy, but while Diaghilev willingly made use of new trends such as cubism, futurism, and constructivism, he never sacrificed the dance to them as did the Swedish Ballet of Rolf de Maré and Jean Borlin in the early nineteen-twenties. *Parade*, a witty work about a circus, may have had scenery and costumes in Picasso's cubist style and a modern score by Erik Satie, but it was nonetheless full of brilliant dancing.

Nijinsky, who was not allowed to visit belligerent countries under the terms of his parole, rejoined the company in neutral Spain. He seemed stranger than ever, and in Barcelona Diaghilev once had to call in the police to prevent him leaving the company without warning. He accompanied the company to South America, and in Buenos Aires in the late summer of 1917, he danced for the last time, at the age of twenty-seven, in *Le Spectre de la Rose* and *Petrushka*, his two greatest roles. Nijinsky's tragedy is one of the most heart-rending in the whole history of ballet. For some time his mental instability had been noticeably on the increase, and when he returned to Europe in the last year of the First World War, his reason finally and irretrievably gave way. For more than thirty years he lived on in the darkness of his mind, tended by his devoted wife, until he died, already a legend, in 1950.

It was no easy matter for an unsubsidized ballet company to survive in a war-torn Europe, and had it not been for Spain and the patronage of King Alfonso, the Diaghilev Ballet would inevitably have succumbed. The early months of 1918 found the company eking out a precarious existence in Spain, and when Diaghilev eventually negotiated a contract for a season in London, the company was on the point of disintegrating. A few dancers had in fact already despaired and left.

To London ballet-goers there were several unfamiliar names on the playbills, for more than four years had passed since the company's last visit. There was no mention of Karsavina and Bolm, and in their place were Lopokova, Tchernicheva, Sokolova (who was really an English girl called Hilda Munnings), Massine, Idzikowski, and Woizikovski. The absence of the favourites of pre-war days was soon overlooked and the season at the London Coliseum was such a success that Diaghilev was able to arrange another London engagement almost immediately afterwards at the Alhambra Theatre, where, in 1919, two of Massine's most successful ballets were given their first performance.

La Boutique Fantasque, a gay work about a toyshop where all the toys come alive, was a triumph almost from the moment the opening bars of Rossini's scintillating score were heard for the first time. It was based on the old Viennese ballet of *The Fairy Doll* which had been revived at the Maryinsky by the Legat brothers early in the century. Bakst had designed that production, and Diaghilev had first of all thought of him for the version he was planning. Then he changed his mind and asked André Derain to design it, and Bakst understandably took the greatest exception. Diaghilev's version was more an original work than a revival, for the only thing that it shared with its prececessor was the idea behind the scenario. He had even discarded the original score, and in its place he had asked Respighi to arrange and orchestrate some of Rossini's pieces he had discovered in an Italian museum. When the ballet was first given in London, Lopokova and Massine brought the house down every night with their cancan, Idzikowski was the Snob and Cecchetti the Shopkeeper, and indeed the cast list included a host of celebrities.

The other new Massine ballet was *The Three-cornered Hat*, with a wonderful score by de Falla and scenery and costumes by Picasso that were brilliantly economical in design. This was the fruit of Massine's observations in Spain, where he had absorbed the essence of Spanish dancing so completely that even Spaniards acknowledged the ballet's authentic flavour. He had learnt much from a remarkable gipsy dancer called Felix, whom Diaghilev brought to London. Unknown to anyone else, Felix was under the illusion that he was to dance in the new ballet, and the discovery that he was not to be its star brought on an attack of madness. Diaghilev was very much affected by this man's tragedy, and he never let a visit to England pass without visiting him at his asylum. Massine had a double triumph in this ballet too. He danced the leading role of the Miller with tremendous presence and received a deafening ovation after his *farucca*. For the older ballet-goers especially, the ballet had another appeal, for it marked the return, in the role of the Miller's wife, of Tamara Karsavina, who had left her native Russia for the last time.

It was soon after this that relations between Diaghilev and his new ballet-master began to worsen, and early in 1921 Massine left the company after producing another successful ballet the year before, *Pulcinella*, to a score by Stravinsky after Pergolesi. Diaghilev was very upset at the loss of Massine, but he soon began to look round for someone else whom he could make into a choreographer. His choice rested on a young dancer called Slavinsky, and he ordered Larionov to instruct him and help him produce a ballet called *The Buffoon*. Despite scenery by Picasso and a score by Prokofiev, it was not a success, and one day, in London, Diaghilev half-jokingly remarked to Grigoriev that he wished he could stage a ballet that would run for ever, like the musical comedy *Chu Chin Chow*. Grigoriev's suggestion of *Coppélia* obviously set Diaghilev thinking, for he often returned to the subject, and then one day he announced that he was going to revive *The Sleeping Beauty*.

To many, the 1921 production of this ballet in London – under the title of *The Sleeping Princess* – must have seemed a revolutionary departure for Diaghilev. His decision was, of course, partly due to his having lost his only choreographer, but in fact he always remained true to the classical tradition, even when promoting the most modern ideas. He always, for instance, laid great importance on there being a good teacher available to give his dancers classes: when Cecchetti left him to take up an official post at La Scala, Milan, Diaghilev engaged Nicolas Legat, and in the company's last years these duties were undertaken by Tchernicheva. In reviving *The Sleeping Princess*, Diaghilev dreamt of bringing back the glories of the Maryinsky, and he placed the production in the hands of Nicolas Sergueyev, who had written down many of the old Maryinsky ballets in the Stepanov system of dance-notation which had been taught in St Petersburg. Baskt was prevailed upon to design the scenery and costumes: it was to be his last work for Diaghilev, for he died soon afterwards. Stravinsky, who was a great admirer of Tchaikovsky, reorchestrated some of the music, while Bronislava Nijinska, Nijinsky's sister, arranged some additional dances.

Diaghilev pinned all his hopes on this splendid production being a success. So much depended on it that when, on the first night, the machinery did not work properly and the enchanted forest refused to grow, he broke down and wept. During its run, no less than four ballerinas danced the part of Princess Aurora. At the first performance it was Olga Spessivtseva (whose name Diaghilev later changed to Spessiva), a young ballerina from the Maryinsky with a fragile beauty and a pure, ethereal style. Cecchetti thought as highly of her as of Pavlova, saying they were like the two halves of an apple, to which Diaghilev, who knew whom he preferred, remarked that Spessivtseva was the half that had seen the sun. Spessivtseva was followed by two Maryinsky ballerinas of Imperial days, Vera Trefilova and Lubov Egorova, and one of Diaghilev's own ballerinas, Lydia Lopokova. Carlotta Brianza, who had danced Aurora when the ballet was first performed at St Petersburg in 1890, returned to the stage in the role of Fairy Carabosse, and at a special performance to mark Cecchetti's golden jubilee, the old man took this part, which he had created, to make his last appearance on the stage. But although it caused a great stir and was an undoubted artistic success, *The Sleeping Princess* did not draw the full houses that Diaghilev had counted on, and it was withdrawn after little more than a hundred performances. Diaghilev was bitterly disappointed. 'This is the last relic of the great days of St Petersburg,' he said sadly to some friends who came to see it just before it was taken off.

The Sleeping Princess was never performed elsewhere because the scenery and costumes were seized by the theatre management on account of the debt that Diaghilev owed on the production. But if the ballet had not solved his financial problem, it had at least presented Diaghilev with a choreographer. In the years to come, Nijinska was to produce a series of ballets for him, the most successful being *Les Noces* in 1923, and two sophisticated little works, *Les Biches* and *The Blue Train*, in 1924. *Les Noces*, which H. G. Wells said was the most interesting ballet he had ever seen, was in every sense a Russian ballet, with music by Stravinsky and scenery and costumes by Goncharova, but the other two, like most of Diaghilev's later productions, were largely French in inspiration. *Les Biches* was a slight, entertaining piece with a witty score by Poulenc and décor by Marie Laurencin, while *The Blue Train* had a scenario by Jean Cocteau and music by Milhaud. As the nineteen-twenties ran their course, Diaghilev's policy developed more and more into a seeking after novelty for novelty's sake, and this was leading him to present ballets which pleased the fancy of the Parisian 'snob' public who applauded anything new, even if they did not understand it, but which have proved to be too frail to last.

The Blue Train, for example, was a superficial work whose

only claim to be remembered is that in it Anton Dolin came into prominence for the first time, dancing a spectacular acrobatic variation as a playboy of a fashionable seaside resort. Dolin, one of a number of promising young dancers who joined Diaghilev in the early nineteen-twenties, was the first British male dancer to gain an international reputation.

Dancers were still joining Diaghilev from Russia, and in 1923 there arrived at Monte Carlo five pupils from Nijinska's school at Kiev. When Diaghilev saw them for the first time, he was so disappointed by their lack of experience that he remarked that it hardly seemed worth the trouble to have brought them such a distance. One of them had arrived unexpectedly in the place of a boy who had vanished when the time arrived for their departure. His name was Serge Lifar, and he worked so hard that Diaghilev eventually encouraged him to go to Italy and study for a while with Cecchetti. When Lifar returned, he had made the most extraordinary progress. With his splendid physique and striking personality, he now had an astonishing technique and a lithe and graceful style. He quickly eclipsed his comrades and became the last great male dancer of the Diaghilev Ballet.

Among the last of the Russian dancers from the old Imperial school to emigrate to Western Europe were Alexandra Danilova and George Balanchine, who joined Diaghilev in 1924. The company remained almost exclusively Russian, however, to the very end, despite the presence of a small number of English dancers. Among these, in addition to Sokolova and Dolin, there were Vera Savina, who was originally Vera Clarke, Massine's first wife, and a young dancer with very decided ideas of her own who became a member of the company for two years in order to gain experience – Ninette de Valois. And finally, in 1925, Diaghilev engaged a small English girl of fifteen called Alicia Marks who was to develop into a ballerina of great charm and – because it was essential to appear to be Russian in Diaghilev's company even if one was a Londoner born and bred – was to adopt the name of Markova.

While in the Diaghilev Ballet's first period it had been the ballets themselves that had made history, the company's later years are now remembered more for the individual dancers who then attracted the public's attention for the first time and who were to influence the course which ballet was to take after Diaghilev's death. Diaghilev himself still directed the artistic policy of the company, but in the last years of his life he became increasingly absorbed in his new hobby of book-collecting. Much of his authority and power he delegated to his secretary, Boris Kochno, whom he hoped would be his successor, and who wrote the scenarios of many of the company's later ballets. As time went by Diaghilev's quest for novelty became more and more fevered. The older he became, the greater was his horror of being old-fashioned. He forgot that nothing grows more quickly out-of-date than the ultra-modern, and ballets like *The Cat*, with its celluloid scenery and costumes, and the Soviet-inspired *Pas d'Acier*, in which the stage was cluttered up with machinery, caused a stir at the time but did not survive.

The choreography of most of the ballets that Diaghilev presented between 1925 and 1929 were by Balanchine, but Massine returned from time to time, and in 1929 Lifar made his début as a choreographer with a revival of *The Fox*. Of Balanchine's ballets, three had English associations. The surrealist ballet, *Romeo and Juliet*, had a score by Constant Lambert who was to play an important part in the growth of the Sadler's Wells Ballet. On the opening night it sparked off a rowdy demonstration, when the left-wing surrealists turned up in force to voice their disapproval of the designers Mirò and Ernst for having worked for a capitalist such as Diaghilev. In the same year, 1926, Balanchine evoked the penny-plain-tuppence-coloured toy theatres of the Victorian era in *The Triumph of Neptune*, which had a scenario by Sacheverell Sitwell and music by Lord Berners. And two years later, a ballet called *The Gods go a-begging* was hurriedly put together in London to some of Handel's music which Sir Thomas Beecham arranged, and turned out to be an unexpected success.

13. Irina Baronova in *Cotillon* (*Merlyn Severn*)

14. Alexandra Danilova in *The Gods go a-Begging* (*Anthony*)

15. Serge Lifar in *Les Créatures de Prométhée* (Lenare)

16. Yvette Chauviré (*Houston Rogers*)

17. Roland Petit and Renée Jeanmaire in *Carmen* (*Lido*)

18. Lavrovsky's *Romeo and Juliet*. The Death of Mercutio (*The Times*)

19a. Galina Ulanova
in *Swan Lake*

19b. Alicia Markova
in *Giselle* (*Anthony*)

20. Svetlana Beriosova in *Perséphone* (*Reg Wilson*)

21. Nora Kaye and Hugh Laing in *Pillar of Fire* (*Foto-Semo*)

22. Balanchine's *Agon* (*Fred Fehl*)

23. The tarantella from Bournonville's *Napoli* (*G. B. L. Wilson*)

24. A moment from Robbins's *New York Export: Op. Jazz*

The most important works that Balanchine arranged for Diaghilev were the Stravinsky ballet, *Apollo*, first given in 1928, and *The Prodigal Son*, which was produced the following year and was to be the last creation of the Diaghilev Ballet. *The Prodigal Son* had music by Prokofiev and scenery and costumes by Rouault, who worked so slowly that in the end it was necessary to lock him in his hotel room so that the designs should be ready in time. This ballet was a departure from the superficial works of the twenties and a return to the expressive ballet. Lifar gave a wonderful performance as the Prodigal Son, and the scene of his return to his father's house, dragging himself painfully across the stage, supported by a stave, was supremely moving.

After the summer season in London in 1929, Diaghilev said good-bye to his company and left to spend a holiday in his beloved Venice. There, a few weeks later, he was suddenly taken ill. Kochno and Lifar were at his bedside when he died on 19 August. That night, a violent thunderstorm broke over the city, reverberating like the final chords of a great symphony. A few days later his body was taken across the water in a gondola to be buried in the shade of the cypress trees on the island of San Michele.

CHAPTER EIGHT

Pavlova

THE paths of Diaghilev and Anna Pavlova rarely crossed; in fact, their viewpoints were fundamentally opposed. While it was Diaghilev's ideal to subordinate everything to making ballet a complete work of art in itself, to Pavlova the dance was unquestionably supreme. Their separate achievements were also very different, although when we look back at their life's work, we can see that they were really complementary to one another and that we owe an enormous debt to them both. For while Diaghilev was striving to raise ballet to the level of a major art by inducing the finest artists and musicians to work for him, Pavlova was giving hundreds of thousands of people all over the world their first taste of ballet.

Anna Pavlova came from a very poor peasant family, and was a weak and sickly child. One winter's evening, as a special treat, her mother took her to the Maryinsky to see *The Sleeping Beauty*. The little girl was spellbound, and firmly announced that one day she would herself dance as the Princess. This was far from an idle childhood dream, for from that moment on she did not rest until she made her mother enter her for the Imperial Ballet School. There she worked very hard under Evgenia Sokolova, Gerdt, and Johansson, but she feared that she was under a disadvantage, for being slenderly built, with long and beautifully shaped legs and a wonderfully arched instep, she was far from conforming to the strong physique of Legnani. But wisely Gerdt dissuaded her from attempting to emulate the Italian dancer's technical virtuosity, and as a result, while she mastered the technique, she developed also a quality of delicate and ethereal grace that was to set her apart from all other dancers of her time. In time she began to study under Cecchetti, with whom she was to take classes almost up to his death, and he used to say that she possessed that which can be taught only by God. She made a successful début at the Maryinsky, and in a few years rose to the rank of ballerina.

She was only a year or two younger than Fokine, and often danced with him in those early days. When he was making his early essays in choreography, he found she was a perfect interpreter of his work. For her he arranged a waltz in the little suite of dances called *Chopiniana*, and he wrote afterwards that if she had not danced so marvellously he might never have created *Les Sylphides*. But the most famous work he produced for her was *The Dying Swan*, to the well-known music by Saint-Saëns. He arranged it in only a few minutes, but simple though it was as a composition, it was as near perfect as it was possible for a dance to be. In Fokine's own words, it was a 'combination of masterful technique with expressiveness'. Pavlova was to perform it to the end of her career, and in people's imaginations she was to be associated with the proud bird in its death-struggle in the same way that, generations before, the very mention of the name of Taglioni would conjure up a vision of the Sylphide.

Pavlova's fame began to spread beyond the borders of Russia in 1907, when she made her first European tour with Bolm as her partner, two years before Diaghilev's first season in Paris. Her association with Diaghilev, as we have seen, was brief, and she only danced for him again once after his first season, being distressed not only by the prominence given to Nijinsky, but also – and this was perhaps the more fundamental reason for her leaving him – by the way in which the individuality of the dancers was lost sight of in his ballets. Also, while agreeing with Fokine that the dance should be expressive, she would not admit that music and painting should assume the importance that it did in Diaghilev's productions.

She was essentially a dancer with a mission. 'I want to dance for everybody in the world,' she once said, and during the last twenty years of her life, she went as far as was humanly possible to fulfil this desire. In 1910, with Mordkin as her partner, she had fabulous successes in New York and London. Three years later she resigned from the Maryinsky, which could give her no more scope for her genius than Diaghilev, but by then she had already formed her own company, which, as time went by, included more and more English dancers, whom she found not only proficient but reliable and equable in temperament. Indeed, if such a roving personality as Pavlova can be said to have had a home, it was in England, for she bought a house in Hampstead, where she relaxed and gave classes and spent long hours with her pet swans.

The outbreak of the First World War found her, like Nijinsky, on enemy territory, but she managed to reach England and set out almost at once for the United States. She did not return to Europe until after the war, and spent the intervening years touring North and South America, with Volinine as her partner. In 1916 she stopped in Hollywood to make a silent film of the opera *The Dumb Girl of Portici*. When peace came, she embarked on a hectic round of tours that were to cover the whole world. She visited provincial towns as well as great cities, and brought ballet to places which had never seen it before. In all, she is said to have covered some half a million miles.

Her vitality was almost superhuman. The dance was everything to her, and Sol Hurok, the American impresario who was also a personal friend, thought that it had become impossible for her to live without working, because she had emptied her life of everything else. Indeed, if ever a dancer were dedicated to her art, that dancer was Pavlova. During one of her early tours, before the First World War, when a crowd of admirers had followed her to her hotel in Stockholm, she asked what she could have done to inspire such enthusiasm, and her Russian maid said: 'Madam, you have made them happy by enabling them to forget for an hour the sadnesses of life.' Pavlova was very impressed by these words, which seemed to explain to her the very purpose of her art and indeed of her whole life. This dedication to her art conveyed itself to others through the force of her extraordinary personality, which had a sort of magnetic effect on the audience when she was on the stage. A learned Indian connoisseur of the arts said it was a religious experience to see her dancing, and Uday Shankar and several other pioneers of the recent revival of Indian dancing were directly inspired by her dancing. But it also converted untold numbers to a love of ballet. In no small part the widespread popularity of ballet today is due to Pavlova. Robert Helpmann took up dancing after seeing her in Australia, and thousands of miles away, in Ecuador, she awakened a similar ambition in another boy, Frederick Ashton.

In Pavlova's repertory, it was her dancing that mattered above everything else, not the ballets themselves. She never claimed to bring anything new to ballet; all she wanted was to carry the dance, in its purest form, to the four corners of the earth. Her repertory was therefore unadventurous, consisting largely of revivals of ballets she remembered from her Maryinsky days, solos and *pas de deux*, and new ballets that were remarkable neither for their music, their décor, nor their choreography. Very little of this repertory has survived. *The Dying Swan* is still performed by Markova and Chauviré in the West, and in a different, more heroic version, by Ulanova in Russia; *Autumn Leaves*, Pavlova's own ballet to Chopin music, which she originally danced with Volinine to choreography by Gorsky, has also been revived by Markova; but the other ballets are now no more than memories.

In the end the enormous strain to which she had subjected herself for so many years began to tell, and in January 1931, while travelling to The Hague to embark on another tour, she caught a chill. Pneumonia set in with horrifying rapidity, and in a very short time the news of her death was being flashed across the world, shocking millions by its very unexpectedness. In London, two days later, the Camargo Society was giving its second performance, when Constant Lambert, who was conducting, turned and announced that the orchestra would play *The Dying Swan* in Pavlova's memory. As the music began, the curtain rose to reveal an empty stage on which a single spotlight played. No tribute could have been more moving.

CHAPTER NINE

The Ballets Russes of the Nineteen-Thirties

THE death of Diaghilev dealt ballet a stunning blow. His company disintegrated almost at once, and more than two years went by before any serious attempt was made to resume his life's work. The revival that then took place was due to two men, Colonel de Basil and René Blum, but for different reasons neither was able to exert his authority in the way Diaghilev had done and the story of the Ballet Russe companies of the nineteen-thirties is chequered with intrigues, quarrels, and defections. Before long, what began as a single company split into two, between which there was a continual interchange of dancers. The whole story is, in fact, very complicated and much of it still remains to be written, for many of the passions that were kindled have not cooled even yet. But what these Ballet Russe companies lacked in stability, they made up in glamour, for the stormy background that accompanied them wherever they went made these gipsy-like Russians far more interesting to the public than the more regular development of companies like the Paris Opéra Ballet or the Vic-Wells Ballet. It was this glamour that inspired the setting of Caryl Brahms and S. J. Simon's brilliant comic novel, *A Bullet in the Ballet*.

The company was formed in Monte Carlo in 1932 when Colonel de Basil and René Blum agreed to join forces. These two partners were a very ill-assorted pair. De Basil was a difficult man to work with, inscrutable and unpredictable, who surrounded himself with an almost Oriental web of intrigue, while René Blum was gentle, courteous, and cultured. Between them they built up a strong company with Massine and Balanchine as the principal choreographers, and the invaluable Grigoriev, who had served Diaghilev from the beginning and was said to hold the whole of the Diaghilev repertory in his memory, was engaged as *régisseur*. Many of Diaghilev's dancers had other commitments, but Tchernicheva, Dubrovska, and Woizikovski were free to join, and the company soon produced its own stars in the three 'baby ballerinas', Toumanova, Riabouchinska, and Baronova.

These three girls created an immediate sensation with their prodigious technique and fresh, youthful charm, and many of their admirers were amazed to see them coming out of the stage-door after the performance, with their hair in pigtails, and dressed in short skirts and ankle socks. Tamara Toumanova was a dark, dramatic beauty who had been born in a cattle-truck during her parents' flight from Russia. Irina Baronova was fair, with a piquant expression and a gay and warm personality, while Tatiana Riabouchinska, the only one of them to come from a family of dancers, was blonde and delicate both in feature and movement. All three were discoveries of Balanchine. He had found Toumanova and Baronova studying with Preobrajenska, and Riabouchinska he had noticed in Kshesinska's studio.

The classes of the great Russian teachers who had settled in Paris after the Russian Revolution – Kshesinska, Preobrajenska, Trefilova, Egorova, and Volinine – proved to be fertile nurseries from which many other dancers were recruited for the company. In this way something of the tradition of the old Imperial Russian Ballet was preserved in the West, although direct links with Russia were, to all intents and purposes, broken. What could not be reproduced, however, was the iron discipline that had been instilled in the Imperial school and which Diaghilev, by the force of his personality, had to some extent succeeded in maintaining.

One feature of the Diaghilev Ballet was not to be found in the Ballet Russe companies of the thirties. Blum and de Basil did not consciously aim at shocking the public, as Diaghilev had done, particularly in his later years, and the programmes appealed to a much wider public as a result. This more conservative artistic policy did not mean, however, that the high musical and artistic standards which Diaghilev set were not being followed. Far from it. Auric and Françaix, two of the leading French composers of the younger school, were among those who wrote scores for the company, while the designers included such distinguished names as Alexandre Benois, Natalie Goncharova, André Derain, Christian Bérard, Raoul Dufy, Mariano Andreu, and Joan Miró.

In 1932, the first year of the company's existence, Balanchine produced two important ballets, *La Concurrence* and *Cotillon*, which brought fame to Toumanova. *Cotillon* lingered in the memory of those who saw it because of its haunting atmosphere and its suggestion of adolescent emotions against a background of sophistication. It ended with a staggering series of *fouettés*, which Toumanova performed alone in the centre of the stage, so faultlessly as to cause the same sort of sensation that Zucchi must have created in St Petersburg forty years before: it was her claim that she was the first ballerina to perform thirty-two double *fouettés* and sixteen triple *fouettés* in actual performance.

Massine, for his part, contributed *Jeux d'Enfants*, which was an ideal ballet for the baby ballerinas. At its creation Riabouchinska played the Child with beguiling simplicity and Toumanova was perfectly cast as the Top, but when the company came to London in 1933, it was Baronova's turn to triumph. Replacing Toumanova, she thrilled the English audience with her flashing *fouettés*, performed with bewildering speed and precision.

This London visit was such a success that the engagement was extended from three weeks to four months. Balanchine had by then already left to form his short-lived Ballets 1933, but the company had been strengthened by the addition of Danilova, while Toumanova, who had left with Balanchine, returned to the fold before the season closed. Several new works by Massine had been added to the repertory at Monte Carlo immediately before the company left for London, and two of these were particularly successful. The most important of them was *Les Présages*, which was performed to Tchaikovsky's 5th Symphony, but *Le Beau Danube*, in the version we know today, was perhaps the greater favourite with the public. This was an evocation of Old Vienna to Strauss music, with Massine as the Hussar, Danilova as the Street Dancer, David Lichine as the King of the Dandies, and Baronova as the First Hand.

Les Présages, the first of Massine's symphonic ballets, marked an important development in choreography. There had been a few instances previously of choreographers arranging ballets to symphonies – Beethoven's Pastorale Symphony had twice been used in London in Romantic times, and Alexander Gorsky had arranged a ballet to Glazounov's 5th Symphony – but all these were isolated productions which had no consequence. Massine's *Les Présages*, on the other hand, was to lead to other works of the same kind. He took as his theme the struggle between man and his destiny. Lichine and Woizikovski played the hero and Fate, and Baronova and Riabouchinska had memorable roles as Passion and Frivolity. During the London season, Massine's second symphonic ballet, *Choreartium*, to Brahm's 4th Symphony, was produced.

The company's first American tour followed in the winter of 1933. Preceded by a fantastic barrage of publicity, they enjoyed a great triumph and Massine produced a ballet about the laying of the great railway across America, *Union Pacific*, which was first given in Philadelphia in 1934. Thereafter American tours became a regular feature of the company's schedule, and it is from these visits, as much as anything else, that the current vogue for ballet in America dates.

Massine presented his third and most important symphonic ballet during the company's London season in 1936. This was his interpretation of Berlioz's *Symphonie Fantastique*, with Toumanova in the role of the Beloved and himself as the Poet. More than two years of preparation had gone into the production, for which Christian Bérard designed the scenery and costumes. It was, however, to be the last ballet which Massine was to produce for de Basil, for soon relations between the two men deteriorated, mainly as a result of de Basil's refusal to appoint Massine artistic director. Their difference split the company into two factions, but when Massine made his farewell appearance with them in San Francisco early in 1938 many tears were shed as the dancers drank his health in champagne, and only de Basil seemed to be absent.

Massine was not alone in being unable to get on with de Basil, for René Blum had parted from him some two years before, in 1936, and formed his own company based on Monte Carlo. He secured Vera Nemchinova as principal ballerina, and stole a march on de Basil by engaging Fokine as ballet-master. Since leaving Diaghilev, Fokine had spent most of his time in America and had only recently returned to Europe. Now, in 1936, having joined Blum, he was to create two important ballets: *L'Épreuve d'Amour*, a ballet on a Chinese theme, with music by Mozart and scenery and costumes by Derain; and *Don Juan*, which was danced to the same score that Gluck had composed for Angiolini nearly two centuries before. Of the two, *L'Épreuve d'Amour* was the more successful. This was one of Fokine's happiest creations, a work of exquisite delicacy. Shortly afterwards Fokine left Blum to join de Basil.

In the spring of 1938, when the Monte Carlo company was reorganized with Sergei Denham as managing director, Massine joined it as artistic director. One of his first tasks was to revive his exhilarating sketch of Offenbach's Paris, *Gaîté Parisienne*, with himself as the Peruvian and Nina Tarakanova as the Glove-seller, a role that was soon afterwards taken over and made her own by Danilova.

It was then that a heroic attempt was made by Sol Hurok to combine the two companies. Negotiations began in New York, and by the time that de Basil sailed for Europe, all the difficulties seemed at last to have been removed. Unfortunately the unpredictable de Basil then changed his mind, Massine began to have doubts about relinquishing some of his authority, and the situation became even more confused when de Basil temporarily lost control of his company. Under its new management, this company opened at Covent Garden in

June, while its rival, Massine's company, began its season at Drury Lane in July. It was a feast for the balletomanes, for it was possible, by running the length of Bow Street during the intervals, to see the best ballets in both programmes on the same night. The public's appetite was further whetted by the publicity which the newspapers gave to a lawsuit over the right to perform Massine's ballets.

The main attractions at Covent Garden were two works by Fokine: a new ballet, *Cinderella*, with Riabouchinska; and a version of *Le Coq d'Or* without singers, which Fokine had revived in America the year before, with Riabouchinska as the Golden Cockerel and Baronova as the Queen of Shemakhan. In addition to Riabouchinska and Baronova, the company included Tchernicheva, Nemchinova, and Lichine.

The Blum company at Drury Lane was, if anything, the stronger of the two. Danilova and Toumanova had followed Massine, and Alicia Markova, the Danish dancer Nini Theilade, Serge Lifar, Igor Youskevitch, Frederic Franklin, and young André Eglevsky were also featured. Its ballets included Massine's *Seventh Symphony*, with music by Beethoven and décor by Bérard, which had been created at Monte Carlo a few weeks before; a new work by Massine called *Nobilissima Visione*; and Lifar's percussion ballet *Icare*.

Neither company emerged the victor from this contest, and flushed with their success the two troupes sailed from Europe, the de Basil company, now under the Colonel's control again and known as Original Ballet Russe, being bound for Australia, and the Massine company, the Ballet Russe de Monte Carlo, going westwards to America. Both companies were in Europe the following summer, the last summer of peace. In London the Original Ballet Russe presented Fokine's *Paganini*, which provided Riabouchinska with one of her finest creations, the role of the young Florentine girl who is bewitched by the sounds of Paganini's violin; while in Monte Carlo Massine, in collaboration with the great Spanish dancer Argentinita, produced *Capriccio Espagnol* to Rimsky-Korsakov's music for the Ballet Russe de Monte Carlo.

The outbreak of war in September 1939 found Massine's company in France, where it had just finished a triumphant season in Paris. The dancers heard the news when another dancer burst into one of Massine's rehearsals brandishing a paper. They all wanted to stop and read it, but Massine imposed his authority. 'You will read the paper at the end, not now,' he commanded, and the rehearsal continued until the appointed time.

Shortly afterwards the company left for New York to fulfil an engagement at the Metropolitan. René Blum had not taken an active part in the company's affairs for some time, but the fateful summer of 1940 found him too in New York, though on diplomatic business. With the increasing gravity of the war situation, he felt it his duty to return to his country. After the fall of France, he refused to leave the Occupied Zone while there was still time, preferring to remain in his Paris flat, where he sold his precious books, one by one, to enable himself to live. In 1941 he was arrested by the Germans and taken to the horror camp of Auschwitz, where he died with countless others of his fellow Jews.

Both companies emigrated to America during the war and declined in importance. The Ballet Russe de Monte Carlo, which still exists, has never returned to Europe, but after a brilliant period during the war, when it presented an enormous repertory with Markova, Mia Slavenska, Franklin, Youskevitch, and many other famous dancers, it became more and more an American company, spending most of its time touring the States.

De Basil's Original Ballet Russe had a precarious existence in its latter years. Once, when the company was on its way to South America, the dancers went on strike in Cuba because de Basil cut their salaries. The company managed to survive for some years by touring South America, and after the war, in 1947, enlarged and bolstered up by Sol Hurok, it made a return visit to Europe. This was de Basil's swan-song. Lichine's *Graduation Ball*, a comedy ballet to music by Johann Strauss, had a great success with Lichine and Riabouchinska playing the roles which they had created in Sydney in 1940, but generally the memories of past glories which the company revived were dim and disappointing. Colonel de Basil died after a heart attack in 1951. After his death an attempt was made by George Kirsta to resuscitate the Original Ballet Russe, but the old spirit was dead and the venture almost inevitably failed.

CHAPTER TEN

Contemporary Ballet

THE tradition of ballet is supremely important because the ballet that we see on the stage today has grown out of the history we have recounted in the earlier chapters of this book. The ideas of Noverre and Fokine remain quite as valid as they were when they were first formulated, and we have a more obvious reminder of the significance of tradition in ballet whenever we see *Giselle* or *Swan Lake* or one of the ballets from the Diaghilev period or even from the early years of the Vic-Wells Ballet.

Although ballets can be, and have been, written down in various forms of dance notation, and although methods of teaching have been recorded in great detail, the continuity of this tradition is for the most part handed down from person to person, from ballet-master to dancer at rehearsal, and from teacher to pupil at class. This personal contact gives dancers a direct link with the great figures in ballet's past, for they can trace their technique through their own teacher, their teacher's teacher, and so on, right back to the days when ballet was young. A dancer who has been taught by a pupil of Cecchetti, for example, can trace her lineage back through Lepri, Blasis, Dauberval, Noverre, 'le grand Dupré', Pécour, to Beauchamps himself, who was the first ballet-master of the Paris Opéra in the days of Louis XIV and is reputed to have invented the five positions of the feet.

In this way, the tradition of ballet is not only the concern of writers of history books, but lives on in the ballets that are danced today and in the very technique of the dancers themselves. It is this tradition, in fact, that sets ballet apart from all other forms of dance and gives it a strength and dignity that they lack. What is happening in the world of ballet today will become the history of tomorrow, for the dancers, choreographers, teachers, musicians, and artists who are now working in this medium are enriching this tradition with their own creative ideas, their experiments, and their artistry in performance, and they in turn will hand it on to future generations.

This same tradition nourishes ballet wherever it is performed. For it is fundamentally the same art, even though companies coming from different countries have different styles and different methods of approach. Temperaments and even physique vary from nation to nation, and so do the tastes of the audiences, which are largely fashioned by the sort of ballets to which they are accustomed. Also, other forms of dancing, such as folk-dancing and the modern dance, may influence ballet more in one country than in another. These, and other factors too, go to make up the variations in style which we imply when we speak of 'the French school' or 'the Russian school'. But these are only variations of a single art, and they are in fact all most intimately bound together by the strong threads of tradition. This we shall recognize when we glance at what is being done today in the five main centres of ballet activity – France, Russia, Britain, the U.S.A., and Denmark.

FRANCE

The Diaghilev Ballet, which was sensitive to every new artistic trend which came to the surface in the nineteen-twenties, had a strong and lasting influence on cultured circles in Paris. When French poets, artists, and musicians suddenly discovered it to be a medium in which they could express their ideas, ballet became a very fashionable form of entertainment and inevitably Diaghilev's example was soon followed by other companies. Rolf de Maré's Swedish Ballet, for instance, presented a number of ultra-modernistic ballets by Jean Borlin which caused a certain sensation at the time, and Ida Rubinstein promoted a series of seasons comprising ballets mainly of the exotic type. Later, during the early thirties, Nijinska produced some abstract ballets that in a way foreshadowed the symphonic ballets of Massine, and the companies of de Basil and Blum also paid occasional visits to Paris in the years before the Second World War.

The Paris Opéra did not remain wholly insensible to the new ideas which Diaghilev had let loose, but like most official institutions, it was not prone to sudden change. When Diaghilev first came to Paris, the ballet at the Opéra, despite the presence of Zambelli, had lost much of its former importance, owing largely to the rising prestige of opera. The successes of the Diaghilev Ballet soon began to tip the scales in its favour, but it was not until Jacques Rouché became Director in 1914 that this trend really began to penetrate the Opéra. Rouché had a great understanding of ballet. Previously he had managed the Théâtre des Arts, where he had presented several excellent ballets, including *Istar* and *The Spider's Banquet*, which had superb scores by d'Indy and Roussel respectively, and his long term as Director of the Opéra was to see a vigorous revival of French ballet.

As was to be expected, little important activity took place at the Opéra during the First World War, but after the Armistice, Rouché soon showed that he considered ballet to be an important part of the theatre's activities. On several occasions he invited the Diaghilev Ballet to give their seasons at the Opéra, and in 1921 he engaged Fokine to revive *Daphnis and Chloe* and Pavlova to dance in *The Peri*. By then Zambelli's long career as a ballerina was approaching its close, and in 1924 Rouché made a bold break with tradition by securing the services of the Russian ballerina, Olga Spessivtseva. *Giselle*, which had been out of the repertory of the Paris Opéra for more than fifty years, was revived for her by Nicolas Serguevyev, and she gave a performance that thrilled the spectators with its tragic intensity. Meanwhile, the theatre's resident choreographers, Léo Staats and Nicola Guerra, were kept busy, and to add variety to his programmes, Rouché invited Nijinska as guest choreographer. It was in one of her ballets, *Impressions de Music-Hall*, that Zambelli created her last part before retiring to devote herself to teaching.

When Diaghilev died and his company disbanded in 1929,

the Paris Opéra Ballet had been recovering its strength for some years, but its prestige still stood below that of the opera. Rouché now saw his opportunity, and he engaged Balanchine to produce a ballet to Beethoven's *Creatures of Prometheus*, to which Viganò had arranged a ballet in 1801. Balanchine, however, fell ill and had to abandon the task after the first few rehearsals; as a result the choreography was undertaken by Lifar, whom Rouché had engaged at the same time to dance the leading role.

After *The Creatures of Prometheus*, which was produced at the end of 1929, Lifar became permanently attached to the Opéra as choreographer and principal male dancer, and with one short interval, he was to dominate the ballet there until his departure in 1958. In fact, during this period he brought about a complete transformation. The company's technical qualities remained intact, for Zambelli remained in charge of the school until 1955, but Lifar's example made the dancers much more aware of their vocation. By introducing a breath of the Diaghilev Ballet, which has now become part of the Opéra's tradition, Lifar restored to French ballet its self-respect. With Rouché's support, he insisted on many reforms, such as abolishing the century-old right of the subscribers to go backstage to chat with the dancers before the ballet, but the most significant change of all came when he prevailed upon Rouché to inaugurate weekly performances given over wholly to ballet.

Lifar's first triumphs at the Opéra were due to his talents as a dancer rather than his ability as a choreographer, for his splendid physique, his virile style, and his strong personality made a tremendous impression on the Parisian public. When *Giselle* was revived in 1932, he built up the role of Albrecht so that it was of equal importance to that of Giselle, even though it was Spessivtseva herself who was playing the latter part.

Although the Opéra presented ballets by other choreographers such as Staats and Aveline, it was Lifar who caught the imagination of the public. He was a man of fertile ideas who soon showed that he was unafraid of expressing himself in print, and in 1934 he published *The Manifesto of the Choreographer*, in which he proclaimed his belief that the composer should submit to the choreographer's ideas in the creation of a ballet. The following year, he applied these ideas in *Icare*, which was danced to a purely percussion score written to fit the choreography. As Icarus, the man in Greek legend who tried to fly but approached too close to the sun so that the wax melted on his wings and he fell to his death, Lifar gave a powerful performance which seemed to gain in impact by the unfamiliar accompaniment.

The Second World War was a tragic period for the French, who for four long years had to endure the humiliation of living under the German occupation. Like the English on the other side of the Channel, they turned to ballet as a means of escape, and every Wednesday evening the Opéra was packed by an audience eager to drink in the beauties that the dance had to offer. In the depths of mid-winter, the theatre, though unheated, was just as full as it was in the warm summer months, and the audiences cheerfully ignored the thick woollen stockings that the ballerinas had to wear over their tights.

Lifar was at his most creative during these years, and produced three of his greatest ballets. *Le Chevalier et la Damoiselle* in 1941 and *Joan de Zarissa* of 1942 were both romantic in inspiration. Based on a legend of medieval Burgundy about a princess who each night assumes the form of a hart, *Le Chevalier et la Damoiselle* was a two-act ballet, with a fine score by Gaubert that culminated in a splendid tournament scene in which four knights vie for the lady's favour. *Joan de Zarissa*, which evoked both the refinement and the brutality of the late Middle Ages, was an impressively dramatic work which was unluckily dropped from the repertory at the Liberation because its score was written by a German, Werner Egk. In quite a different style was *Suite en Blanc*, first produced in 1943, a classical *divertissement* to a selection from Lalo's score for *Namouna*, which admirably displayed the technical resources of the company.

The company was remarkably strong during these years. Lifar himself was still at the height of his powers as a dancer, as too was Serge Peretti, while three brilliant ballerinas were consolidating their reputations: Solange Schwarz, one of the most enchanting Swanildas in *Coppélia*; Lycette Darsonval, a tall blonde dancer of athletic build who excelled in *Sylvia*; and the greatest of them all, Yvette Chauviré, who was nominated a star dancer after her extraordinary triumph in Lifar's version of *Istar*.

When the Allies liberated Paris in 1944, Lifar, Schwarz, and Chauviré left the Opéra. Lifar and Chauviré were to return before very long, but Schwarz danced only once more on the scene of her former triumphs, when she returned to give her farewell performance in *Coppélia* in 1957. During Lifar's absence, the Opéra Ballet went through a lean period until Balanchine came in 1947 to produce four ballets, including one new work, the glittering *Palais de Cristal*, danced to Bizet's Symphony in C.

Later that year, Lifar returned to the Opéra, but at first only as choreographer. Until he left the second time in 1958, he produced many more ballets, the first being *Les Mirages*, with music by Sauguet, a work which had been in preparation and even had its dress rehearsal just before the Allies entered Paris in 1944, but was not publicly performed until 1947. It tells of a young man who pursues dreams, riches, and love, only to discover they are all mirages and to find himself alone with his shadow. The part of the young man, which Lifar had originally planned for himself, was danced by Michel Renault, while the role of the shadow has been taken with equal success by Yvette Chauviré and Nina Vyroubova, who each in their own way have showed a great understanding of Lifar's choreography. *Phèdre*, produced in 1950, was a very different work. Conceived by Jean Cocteau, with a strong score by Auric, it contained a superb tragic role for Toumanova, who was appearing at the Opéra as guest artist. Shortly before his departure, Lifar produced a ballet that ranks with his most inspired creations, *Les Noces Fantastiques*, with music by Delannoy. It had a Celtic setting, and its poetic plot was conveyed with gripping intensity by Peter Van Dijk and Nina Vyroubova.

Latterly, Lifar had to share the production of new ballets with the Danish choreographer, Harald Lander, who was engaged by the Opéra in 1951. However, only one of Lander's ballets – a revival of *Études* – has really been a success, and from Lifar's departure in 1958 until 1961, the post of ballet-master was held by George Skibine. The Paris Opéra Ballet went into a decline during these years, the only significant addition to the repertory being a full-length version of *Swan Lake* by Bourmeister, the ballet-master of the Moscow Stanislavsky Theatre.

Today the company is led by Christiane Vaussard, Madeleine Lafon, Claude Bessy, Josette Amiel, Claire Motte, Jacqueline Rayet, Youly Algaroff, Jean-Paul Andérani, Peter Van Dijk, Flemming Flinde, and Attilio Labis. Its diminished repertory consists almost entirely of works created since 1930, many of them by Lifar, but with a scattering of ballets that have survived from the nineteenth century. In Paris, the classics are very much less in demand than they are in London. *Giselle*, which was considered old-fashioned in Diaghilev's time, has been restored to favour, but in the version given in St Petersburg at the turn of the century. *Coppélia* has kept its place in the repertory ever since 1870, and probably retains much of Saint-Léon's original choreography, and *Sylvia* and *The Two Pigeons* are also occasionally performed, but in later versions, for both were out of the repertory for long periods at a stretch. Since the war, the company has embarked on a number of foreign tours, and in 1958 it had the distinction of being the first foreign company to appear on the stage of the Bolshoi Theatre in Moscow.

During the bitter years of the occupation, Monte Carlo had provided a haven for many French dancers. In 1942 a company was formed there called the Nouveaux Ballets de Monte Carlo, with Julia Sedova, the former Maryinsky ballerina, and Gustave Ricaux in charge of the classes, and Ludmilla Tcherina, Geneviève Kergrist, Marie-Louise Didion, and Gérard

Mulys among the principal dancers. After the Liberation, another company was formed bearing a very similar name, the Nouveau Ballet de Monte Carlo. Lifar, who was then temporarily ousted from his position at the Paris Opéra, became artistic director and principal choreographer, and produced three important new ballets, *Dramma per Musica*, to music by Bach, *Chota Roustaveli*, and *Nautéos*. The company was very strong in its early days, its dancers including at one time or another Lifar himself, Yvette Chauviré, Renée Jeanmaire, Janine Charrat, Ludmilla Tcherina, Wladimir Skouratoff, Alexandre Kalioujny, and Youly Algaroff. The first phase in its history ended in 1947 when Lifar returned to the Opéra and the company was taken over by the Marquis de Cuevas.

We shall tell of this company's more recent history later on in this section, but meanwhile we must return to Paris, where great events were taking place in the years just after the Liberation. During the occupation, two promising young dancers of the Opéra, Roland Petit and Janine Charrat, had gained a wide following through their dance recitals, and in 1944, feeling thoroughly frustrated at the Opéra, Roland Petit sent in his resignation. He then began to collect round him a number of young dancers, who in time were to form the nucleus of his own company, the Ballets des Champs-Élysées. With Boris Kochno as its artistic director, and with the sympathy and support of Christian Bérard and Jean Cocteau, this company gave its first performance in the autumn of 1945.

Jean Cocteau boldly proclaimed that these young dancers were about to revive the work of Diaghilev, and time was to prove that this prophecy was not wholly unjustified, for during the company's brief existence it raised the prestige of French ballet to a height it had never attained before in recent times. Kochno's experienced artistic direction, Petit's brilliance as a choreographer, and the freshness and youth of the dancers all combined to make a tremendous impact, not only on Paris but also on London, where in the summer of 1946 they brought a welcome touch of glamour to the war-worn city. Most of the company's dancers were at first unknown to the public, and many were little more than children, but their names were soon on everybody's lips: Petit himself, Jean Babilée, Youly Algaroff, Renée Jeanmaire, Nina Vyroubova, Colette Marchand, Irène Skorik, and, the youngest of them all, Ethery Pagava, who was only thirteen when she entered Petit's company in 1945.

Roland Petit produced a succession of memorable ballets for the Ballets des Champs-Élysées. One of his earliest works was a study of a group of wandering circus folk, *Les Forains*, which was designed by Bérard and danced to a score by Sauguet. It was an object-lesson in creating effect with a minimum of means, and few ballets have conveyed such a deeply felt pathos. A little later, he produced another masterpiece, this time in collaboration with Cocteau and the designer Wakhevitch, *Le Jeune Homme et la Mort*. Its sordid theme – the driving of a young artist to suicide by a mysterious girl's cruel disdain – was in the most violent contrast with the music used. The ballet was the result of an extraordinary experiment. It had been rehearsed to popular modern music, and it was only on the day of the première that the dancers learnt that the music to be used was Bach's Passacaglia in C minor. Throughout its first performance, Roland Petit was nervously watching from the wings and praying that the music would prove long enough. But all was well, and with Jean Babilée and Nathalie Philippart in the two roles, it was acclaimed as a work of tremendous force.

Another important landmark in the company's history was the revival of the old Romantic ballet, *La Sylphide*, with the original music by Schneitzhoeffer. Gsovsky's choreography was new, but conceived in the spirit of the ballet's period, and Nina Vyroubova and Irène Skorik each triumphed in the title-role. One of the company's last successes, before it disbanded in 1950, was a ballet by Lichine called *Creation*, which was danced in practice clothes to total silence.

Meanwhile, in 1947, Roland Petit had left the Ballets des Champs-Élysées after a difference with the management, and formed another company, the Ballets de Paris. In 1948 this company opened its first season in Paris, with Margot Fonteyn appearing as guest artist in a new ballet by Petit with music by Françaix, *Les Demoiselles de la Nuit*, in which she played the part of a cat. But the two ballets by Petit which are most associated with the fitful existence of the Ballets de Paris are *Carmen*, which proved so popular that the company used to advertise its programme as 'Carmen and three other ballets', and *Le Loup*. In both these ballets Roland Petit had the collaboration of a brilliant designer. *Carmen*, which was inspired by the opera and used a selection from Bizet's score, much to the disgust of some of the more conservative French music critics, was designed by Clavé and made Renée Jeanmaire, who played Carmen, a star overnight. *Le Loup* – in which Roland Petit and later Jean Babilée gave memorable performances as the hunted man-wolf and Violette Verdy portrayed the girl who loves him – had sets and costumes by Carzou which caused a sensation with their brilliant colouring and delicate draughtsmanship.

Roland Petit's wartime partner, Janine Charrat, also developed into a choreographer with original ideas. For her own company, the Ballets de France, she staged a brilliant ballet about the inmates of a lunatic asylum, *Les Algues*, and she created another important ballet, *Abraxas*, for the Berlin State Opera. Her career came near to ending in tragedy in 1961, when her costume caught fire during a television rehearsal of *Les Algues*. Terribly burned, she was only saved by the resources of modern medicine and her own indomitable courage.

Drawn away from classical ballet, in which he received his training, towards modern dance and *avant-garde* trends, Maurice Béjart has produced a number of experimental works in the jumble of recorded sounds that is known as *musique concrète*. His best-known ballet of this kind is *Symphonie pour un Homme Seul*, first performed in 1955, which explored the solitude of modern man. He is now ballet-master at the Théâtre de la Monnaie, Brussels, where in 1959 he staged a powerful new version of *The Rite of Spring*.

Jean Babilée has also launched out as a choreographer, one of his most successful works being *Balance à Trois*, and Peter Van Dijk, too, has shown promise in this direction, particularly with his rendering of Schubert's Unfinished Symphony.

A survey of French ballet today would be incomplete without mention of the Ballet International de la Marquise de Cuevas, which, though not strictly a French company, has nevertheless become an integral part of the ballet scene of Paris, where it gives regular seasons and has attracted an enthusiastic following. Its popularity, however, extends throughout the Continent, and its performances are a favourite attraction at fashionable pleasure resorts such as Monte Carlo, Cannes, Deauville, and Biarritz.

The company's creator, the Marquis de Cuevas, was a character who might have stepped out of another age, for a Spanish nobleman with his own private ballet company seemed strangely out of place in this modern world. Being married to a granddaughter of John D. Rockefeller, the American millionaire, he was independent of financiers and able to indulge his consuming love for the ballet to the full. His company's history dates back to 1944, when his first ballet venture, Ballet International, gave a single season in New York. He lost a great deal of money, but this did not deter him from acquiring three years later the Nouveau Ballet de Monte Carlo, whose repertory he was able to swell with the ballets created for Ballet International. To give further strength to the new company, he brought over from America a number of dancers, including Rosella Hightower, Marjorie Tallchief, André Eglevsky, and George Skibine.

Since 1947 the company has been remarkably stable in its upper ranks. Hightower, a ballerina of unusual technical brilliance, has been its principal star ever since its formation, and Skibine and Tallchief only left in 1957 when they were engaged at the Paris Opéra. Another dancer who has been with the company since the beginning is Serge Golovine, who has developed into one of the most sensationally gifted male dancers of the present generation. More recently the company has been strengthened by the engagement of dancers whose reputations had been established with state companies. From the Paris Opéra came Nina Vyroubova and Liane Daydé, and in 1961 Paris flocked to see the astonishing Rudolf Nureyev, who was engaged after he had defected from the Kirov Ballet during its tour of Western Europe.

In the dozen years or so of its existence, the company has presented many ballets, most of which have been new works. Massine, Nijinska, Balanchine, Lifar, Lichine, Lander, Gsovsky, Milloss, Charrat, and Cranko have all been engaged at one time or another as guest choreographers, and John Taras and George Skibine have each added several ballets to the repertory. Taras' *Piège de Lumière*, with its richly coloured costumes by Levasseur and descriptive score by Damase, was produced in 1952. It contains a wonderful role for Hightower, and is probably the finest ballet the company has produced. Among Skibine's works, in which he and Marjorie Tallchief have been featured, the most successful have been *Annabel Lee* and *Idylle*, but his more ambitious *Prisoner of the Caucasus*, with music by Khatchaturian, has kept its place in the repertory for several years.

The Marquis departed this life with a flourish that was typical of him. Mortally stricken with cancer, he gave the world a farewell taste of his munificence by presenting *The Sleeping Beauty* in its entirety, with settings and costumes of staggering splendour, designed by his nephew Raymond de Larrain. When he died in 1961, the company's days at first seemed numbered, but his widow and his nephew decided to carry on, encouraged by the success of *The Sleeping Beauty*.

Paris is the spiritual home of many dancers. It holds a special place in the history and tradition of ballet, and the tempo of its artistic activity is a constant source of stimulation to anyone with an intelligent and receptive mind. But what attracted dancers there more than anything else in the recent past was the presence of great Russian teachers who emigrated to Paris after the Revolution. Several generations of dancers gratefully perfected their art in Paris under the wise instruction of Preobrajenska, Kshesinska and Egorova, who generously handed on the great traditions of the old Maryinsky. Now their mantle has passed to other, younger teachers, who are today playing their part in maintaining the prestige of Paris as one of the important capitals in the world of dance.

RUSSIA

As a result of the Russian Revolution in 1917, Diaghilev's influence hardly touched ballet in Russia, where its development has consequently been very different to that of ballet in Western Europe and America. Nevertheless, Russian ballet today is very firmly based on tradition. It is, in fact, the direct descendant of the Imperial Russian Ballet, and the great ballet schools of Leningrad and Moscow take great pride in their long and unbroken history – going back, in Leningrad, to 1738 and, in Moscow, to 1773.

Under the Tsars, the main centre of ballet in Russia was St Petersburg, but today Moscow has not only become the nation's capital but has also acquired equal, if not greater, prominence in the realm of ballet. Its importance as a theatrical centre began around the turn of the century, when the Moscow Art Theatre was founded, the great bass Chaliapine made his first appearance, and artists of the modern school such as Golovine and Korovine began working for the theatre. At about the same time, the ballet company of the Bolshoi Theatre, which had been greatly reduced in 1882, was restored to its former strength and given a brilliant young ballet-master, Alexander Gorsky. Gorsky, who was trained in St Petersburg where he was a contemporary of Fokine, was very much influenced by Stanislavsky and the Moscow Art Theatre. He insisted on the importance of dramatic expression and made his dancers live their parts in much the same way that the actors of the Moscow Art Theatre did under Stanislavsky.

Economic difficulties, then the war, and finally the Revolution and the chaos that followed had a serious effect on ballet in Russia, which was still further weakened by the loss of many of its best dancers to join Diaghilev. Indeed, in the early years of the Soviet régime, there was a considerable danger that ballet might be jettisoned as being too closely linked with the pleasures of Tsarist times, and one critic even announced: 'Ballet will now die, for where can such an exotic flower bloom but in the hot-houses of the Court!'

Ballet did survive, however, thanks largely to those teachers who lovingly and courageously preserved intact the great classical tradition: notably Agrippina Vaganova in Leningrad and Vasili Tikhomirov in Moscow. Their task was not an easy one, for in the high passions of those days there was a strong movement to discard the very fundamentals of ballet and create a new form of dance that would express modern life, and appeal to mass audiences. What the extremists overlooked, of course, was that it was not the fundamentals of ballet that were sterile, but the manner in which they had been applied. The upholders of the classical school, on the other hand, saw the problem in a much clearer light. They maintained that the art of ballet had been founded and built up over the centuries on the possibilities of the human body in movement and repose, and that all that was needed was to give ballet a new sense of direction and a greater meaning.

The clash between these two schools of thought continued for some years. One of the leading figures of the extreme modernists was Kasyan Goleizovsky, who produced a number of experimental ballets in the nineteen-twenties. Goleizovsky was experimenting with cubism and constructivism on the concert stage in Moscow at the same time that Diaghilev was toying with the latest modernistic trends of Paris, and it was Diaghilev's hope – a vain one, as it turned out – that Goleizovsky might one day produce a ballet for his company.

Most of the ballets produced in Russia in the nineteen-twenties have now been forgotten, but one work remains – *The Red Poppy*, which was produced in Moscow by Tikhomirov and Lashchiline in 1927. It was the first Russian ballet to have a heroic modern theme, and told of Russian sailors championing Chinese coolies in a treaty port. Although its theme was propagandist and its choreography conventional and even unadventurous, it is important because it marked the victory of the classical school and indicated the course that was to be followed in the years to come. The sailors' dance in the first act, the *yablochko*, danced to a popular song, brought the house down at every performance and started a vogue for that kind of dance on the vaudeville stage. The part of Tao Hoa, a Chinese actress, was created by Ekaterina Geltzer, who had been the prima ballerina of the Bolshoi since before the Revolution.

By then, it was realized that the Russian public was not interested in modernistic experiments which they did not understand, and as a result the classical ballets of old enjoyed a new popularity. At the same time, the champions of the classical school saw their struggle fully justified by the débuts in Leningrad of two brilliant young dancers – Marina Semyonova, who made her first appearance in 1925, and Galina Ulanova, who emerged from the school in 1928.

Once the experimental phase had worked itself out, ballet in Russia began to develop along more orthodox and traditional lines. The desire to make ballet acceptable to a much wider public, however, produced an approach to its problems that differed greatly to that which was followed in Western Europe. The full-length ballet remained the set framework for new works, and scenarios were fashioned to fit this framework. As a result, ballets in Russia invariably have a strong story, which Soviet choreographers, following the tradition of Gorsky more than any other ballet-master of the past, try to convey in a convincing manner by means of dance, mime, and realistic staging. The process of broadening ballet's appeal has also led to another distinguishing feature of contemporary Russian ballet – a much greater use of folk-dance to enrich the choreographer's vocabulary.

Much of the prestige which Russian ballet enjoys today is due to Galina Ulanova. In common with Diaghilev and Pavlova, she had her first experience of ballet when she was taken as a child to see *The Sleeping Beauty* at the Maryinsky. She entered the ballet school there in the years of confusion that followed the Revolution, when many of the pupils had to endure hunger and cold. From the class of her mother, who was a teacher there, she passed under the charge of Vaganova, one of the finest teachers of modern times, who prepared her for her début in 1928. From that moment on, throughout her long career, she has been an important force in Soviet ballet, and today she has become, in the eyes not only of Russians but of the whole world, its very symbol. Many of the great ballets produced in Russia during the past thirty years have been enriched by her portrayal of the leading roles, and her interpretation of Giselle ranks among the greatest of all time.

Ulanova's career coincides with a revival of Russian ballet that is not associated with any one ballet-master, as in the days of Petipa, but by a whole school of choreographers – Lopukhov, Vainonen, Zakharov, Lavrovsky, Chabukiani, Bourmeister, and others. By a remarkable coincidence, this revival began at about the same time that similar revivals were taking place elsewhere: in France, under the influence of Lifar – in Denmark, under Lander – in England, where the Vic-Wells Ballet had recently been formed – and in America, where ballet was about to become popular through the early visits of Colonel de Basil's Ballet Russe.

Until the outbreak of the Second World War, the main centre of activity in Russian ballet was Leningrad, where in 1932 Vasili Vainonen's *Flames of Paris*, with music by Asafiev, was given its first performance. Conceived and produced on an epic scale, it told the story of the French Revolution, and its real hero was the revolutionary mob for whom the choreographer produced some very effective, realistic crowd scenes. Vainonen also drew heavily on folk-dancing, and introduced a number of French regional dances in his choreography. Two years later, still in Leningrad, Rostislav Zakharov produced *The Fountain of Bakhshisarai*, which also had a score by Asafiev. The story of this ballet was taken from Pushkin's lyric about a Polish girl, Maria, who is captured by a Tartar khan and is stabbed by a jealous favourite. The fountain of the story is erected to her memory, and the khan is last seen disconsolately listening to the water as it falls, like teardrops, to the ground. The realistic manner in which the action was unfolded was very effective, and Ulanova gave a deeply moving performance in the role of Maria.

Towards the end of the thirties, two successful ballets were produced in Leningrad by the great male dancer, Vakhtang Chabukiani: *The Heart of the Hills* in 1938, and *Laurencia* in 1939. Chabukiani is a Georgian, and the first of these ballets had a Georgian theme. As a choreographer, he showed great originality in the way in which he dispensed with mime and expressed the action in the dance. In *Laurencia*, which had a Spanish setting, he gave great prominence to the *corps de ballet* and cleverly combined classical ballet technique with the Spanish dance.

The spate of activity in Leningrad continued unabated, and in 1940 Feodor Lopukhov, the brother of Lydia Lopokova, produced *Taras Bulba*, based on a novel by Gogol, and Leonide Lavrovsky's *Romeo and Juliet* – the greatest ballet to have been produced during the Soviet régime – was given its first performance. It was a masterly adaptation of the Shakespeare tragedy, produced on a sumptuous scale to a rich score by Prokofiev, and enhanced by Ulanova's unforgettable creation of the role of Juliet. Every shade of the character was brought out in her interpretation, which was none the less complete despite the lack of Shakespeare's lines.

In the summer of 1941, all this activity was brutally interrupted by the German invasion of Russia, which resulted in both the Leningrad and Moscow companies being evacuated to places of greater safety. The company from the Kirov Theatre in Leningrad went to Perm – the same town where Diaghilev had spent many of his childhood years – while the Bolshoi company from Moscow settled in Kuibyshev. Few new works were presented during this evacuation, the only one of any note being Nina Anismova's *Gayaneh*, to music by Khatchaturian, which she produced at Perm in 1942. During the long siege of Leningrad, the Kirov Theatre was very seriously damaged by shellfire. It was one of the first buildings which the people of Leningrad began to repair, but by the time it was reopened in 1944, its greatest ballerina, Ulanova, had joined the Bolshoi company in Moscow.

Until the war, the Bolshoi Theatre had stood second in importance to the Kirov and had largely built up its modern repertory with revivals of ballets which had already been successfully given in Leningrad, such as *Flames of Paris, The Fountain of Bakhshisarai*, and *Romeo and Juliet*. While this practice has continued since the war, the prestige of the Bolshoi has increased considerably. It was there, in 1945, that Zakharov's *Cinderella*, for which Prokofiev had written his second full-length ballet score, was first produced, with Olga Lepeshinskaya in the title-role. *The Tale of the Stone Flower*, Prokofiev's last ballet – completed only a very short time before his death – was also created at the Bolshoi, where it was staged by Lavrovsky in 1954, with Ulanova as Katerina and Maya Plisetskaya, a brilliant ballerina of a younger generation, as the Mistress of the Copper Mountain. This fairy-tale ballet has since been produced, first in Leningrad in 1957 and in Moscow in 1959, in a new and much more successful version by Yuri Grigorovitch.

The Bolshoi Ballet, which has gained considerable inter-national fame through the cinema and its foreign tours, is remarkably strong both in numbers and in quality. It is headed by two ballerinas of widely differing styles – the poetic Ulanova and the sparkling, extrovert Lepeshinskaya – with another established star in Plisetskaya, and Raisa Struchkova increasingly coming to the fore, while among the male dancers of note are Yuri Zhdanov, Nicolas Fadeyechev, and the outstanding character dancer, Georgi Farmanyantz.

Leningrad has been very active since the war, and its citizens still claim that its ballet leads Moscow in questions of novelty and taste. Since the reopening of the Kirov, a number of important works have been added to its repertory. Za-kharov's *The Bronze Horseman*, another ballet based on a Pushkin poem, with music by Gliere, was presented there in 1949, with Natalia Dudinskaya, who succeeded Ulanova as prima ballerina, in the leading role. It ended with one of those magnificent stage effects in which the Russians excel – a realistic illusion of the River Neva bursting its banks. Leonide Jacobson's *Spartacus*, produced in 1956 with music of Khatchaturian, was a spectacular tale of ancient Rome, while Constantine Sergueyev chose a more contemporary theme, that of race relations in South Africa, when he staged *The Path of Thunder* to a score by Karaev in 1957. Recently a young choreographer of promising talent has emerged in Igor Belsky, whose *Seventh Symphony*, using music by Shostakovitch, was inspired by the heroic defence of besieged Leningrad.

Carrying on its two-centuries-old tradition, the Kirov has continued to produce outstanding young dancers. It was a great tribute to its school that when Rudolf Nureyev left the company after his personal triumph in Paris, the strength of its male dancing seemed in no way impaired when it appeared in London. A company that produces such wonderful young dancers as Yuri Soloviev, Irina Kolpakova, Alla Sizova, and Inna Zubkovskaya commands the very highest respect.

The Bolshoi Ballet and the Kirov Ballet are not the only important Russian companies to have been seen in Western Europe, for in 1956 the Stanislavsky Theatre Ballet from Moscow paid a very successful visit to Paris. Most of this company's ballets have been produced by its ballet-master, Vladimir Bourmeister, whose version of *Swan Lake* is the only one to make use of the full score as Tchaikovsky originally wrote it. It aroused great interest in both Russia and Paris, particularly for the more theatrical treatment of the action, and Ulanova herself, while making several reservations, has praised its originality. One of the recent ballets which Bourmeister has produced for this company is *Joan of Arc*, which was first performed in 1957.

No longer is ballet in Russia confined to the two great cities of Moscow and Leningrad, and already significant work is being done by the many younger companies which have been established in cities and towns all over the Soviet Union. In Tiflis, for example, the capital of Georgia, the ballet is directed by Chabukiani, who in 1957 produced a great Shakespearean epic, *Othello*, in which he himself gave a performance of astonishing power as the Moor.

All this widespread activity has been made possible by the superb system of training which was built up in the old former Imperial schools and has been continued and developed without interruption. This training has produced dancers with a fluidity of movement which courses through the whole body – it is most marked in the Russians' superb *épaulement*, a weak point in Western training – and an inner conviction which enables them to identify themselves with whatever part, important or minor, they are playing. The difference between the schools of Leningrad and Moscow still persists but is not so marked as it used to be, for a single method of teaching has been adopted which Vaganova herself has recorded in her important book, *Basic Principles of Classical Ballet*. These two schools do much more than supply the Bolshoi and Kirov theatres with dancers, for only the best pupils are accepted there, but the others are always certain of a place in one of the smaller opera houses or in one of the numerous folk-dance companies such as the Moiseyev and Beriozka Ensembles.

The isolation of Russian ballet from that of Western Europe and America is at last ending with the exchange visits now being organized, and many lessons may be learned on both sides in the years to come.

BRITAIN

Ballet was popular in London long before there was any thought of establishing a national ballet company in Britain. For more than a century it shared the bills at the Opera House in the Haymarket, and after that, in the fifty years before the First World War, it became the most important feature in the programmes at the Alhambra and Empire music halls in Leicester Square. Later still, the Diaghilev Ballet and Anna Pavlova were always sure of a warm welcome whenever they appeared in London. However, more than an enthusiastic public was needed to establish an English ballet company on a firm footing, the main obstacle being the lack of good schools. One of the few fine dance teachers to open a school in London before 1900 was Édouard Espinosa, who was to play an important part in the founding of the Association of Operatic Dancing in 1920. This organization, which later became the Royal Academy of Dancing, and the Cecchetti Society, which was founded soon afterwards to perpetuate Cecchetti's teaching method, brought about a rapid improvement in the standards of teaching. The result was not only a supply of good dancers but, equally important, the nucleus of a knowledgeable audience.

British ballet as we know it today owes much to the lifework of three great women. The name of Dame Adeline Genée, for long the prima ballerina of the Empire Theatre, is associated with the Royal Academy of Dancing, whose first President she was for more than thirty years. Dame Ninette de Valois' monument is the Royal Ballet organization, while Dame Marie Rambert is the founder of the company which bears her name and which has made a vital contribution to our national ballet.

Marie Rambert studied classical ballet after she left Diaghilev with Cecchetti and a well-known Russian teacher, Serafina Astafieva, and in 1920 she opened her own school in Notting Hill Gate. Six years later she was responsible for the first stirring of British ballet when she encouraged a young man called Frederick Ashton, who had come to her school after studying for a time with Massine, to produce a short ballet in a revue at the Lyric Theatre, Hammersmith. This modest work, *A Tragedy of Fashion*, was so successful that Diaghilev, who was in London at the time, went to see it twice. It was to become historic not only through being Ashton's first ballet, but also because it marked the start of another career, that of the brilliant designer Sophie Fedorovitch.

Marie Rambert's pupils were giving occasional performances in her Notting Hill Gate studio for some time before she founded the Ballet Club in 1930. The Ballet Club was to be one of the most important manifestations of British ballet throughout its formative years in the nineteen-thirties. Marie

Rambert had a remarkable flair for bringing out a young choreographer's talent, and Frederick Ashton, Antony Tudor, and Andrée Howard all learnt many valuable lessons on the tiny stage of her studio, which was later to be transformed into the Mercury Theatre. The very smallness of this stage made attention to detail and subtlety essential if a ballet was to succeed, and a number of exquisite works resulted. In the first year of the Club's existence, Ashton produced his *Capriol Suite*, a set of Elizabethan dances arranged to the airs in Thoinot Arbeau's old book, *Orchésographie*. Among Tudor's ballets were *Jardin aux Lilas*, which he staged to music by Chausson in 1936, a subtle work that suggested the emotions felt by four young people in a moonlit garden, and his deeply moving *Dark Elegies* of the following year, which was a study of mourning set in a fishing village and danced to a song cycle by Mahler. And in 1939 Andrée Howard produced a memorable ballet based on David Garnett's novel, *Lady into Fox*.

While encouraging these young choreographers to produce new ballets, Marie Rambert always kept the importance of tradition well in mind, and although the minute Mercury stage was a far cry from the broad expanses of the Maryinsky, she included excerpts from the classics in her programmes from the very beginning. She also persuaded Karsavina and Woizikovski to appear with her dancers during the early seasons of the Club, and Alicia Markova danced regularly at the Mercury between 1931 and 1935. Soon the Ballet Club was producing some remarkable young dancers who became favourites with the small but staunch audiences of enthusiasts who packed the Mercury Theatre on club nights: the exceptionally beautiful Pearl Argyle, the versatile Diana Gould, the serene and expressive Maude Lloyd, the fay Sally Gilmour, Harold Turner, Walter Gore, Hugh Laing, and Frank Staff. To these dancers ballet was a real vocation, and they cheerfully accepted the small salaries that was all that could be paid them. Throughout the Club's existence, however, there was a continual and understandable exodus of dancers to better-paid jobs with larger organizations.

Shortly before the war Antony Tudor left Rambert to found his own company, London Ballet, for which he produced several new ballets, including his amusing satire about three ballerinas from Russia, France, and Italy – *Gala Performance*. Not long after Dunkirk, London Ballet ceased to exist as an independent unit, but its last creation – Andrée Howard's exquisite *La Fête Étrange*, to music by Fauré – was happily preserved by the Ballet Rambert, with which it merged, and is now in the repertory of the Royal Ballet.

We must now retrace our steps to tell the story of Ninette de Valois and her company. In 1926, at about the same time that Frederick Ashton was preparing his first ballet, de Valois, who had just left Diaghilev, opened a school of ballet in South Kensington which she called the Academy of Choreographic Art. She saw this as the necessary first step towards fulfilling her ambition to found a ballet company of her own, and she lost no time in talking Lilian Baylis, the manager of the Old Vic, into engaging her to stage the dances for the plays there. This was the beginning of a close association between the two women which only ended when Lilian Baylis died. Lilian Baylis understood what de Valois was working towards and gave her all the help and encouragement that lay within her power. When the Sadler's Wells Theatre was reopened in 1931, she accepted de Valois' offer to transfer her school to the theatre in return for the establishment of a permanent ballet company, and thus was formed the Vic-Wells Ballet, which began by appearing at both theatres but soon became attached solely to Sadler's Wells. In the meantime, however, another important development had occurred.

This was the foundation of the Camargo Society with the object of presenting ballet performances at West End theatres three or four times a year. Between 1930 and 1933 it presented a number of new ballets, which were specially commissioned from British choreographers and designers, and two of these, both originally produced in 1931, are still given today: Frederick Ashton's amusing *Façade*, to the music of William Walton, and Ninette de Valois' *Job*, an inspired and faithful transcription for the stage of William Blake's illustrations to the Book of Job, with a specially composed score by Vaughan Williams. The dancers who took part in the Camargo Society performances mostly came from the Ballet Club and the Vic-Wells Ballet, but they were joined from time to time by several eminent guest artists. Dolin and Markova were generous in their support, Spessivtseva came over from Paris to play *Giselle*, and Lopokova returned to dance in *Coppélia*.

By 1933 the Camargo Society had fulfilled its purpose. It had given British ballet a prestige that enabled the Vic-Wells Ballet to withstand the competition from de Basil's Ballet Russe de Monte Carlo, which came to London that year for the first time. The Camargo Society performances were therefore discontinued, and because the Vic-Wells Ballet was the only company in London capable of preserving its more ambitious productions, the Society offered its resources to the young organization.

Throughout the nineteen-thirties the Vic-Wells Ballet went from strength to strength. In de Valois it was fortunate to possess a leader with a genius for organization and the vision to see clearly what the company should aim at. But there was also another important influence at work. In 1932 Constant Lambert became musical director of the company, and from then until his untimely death in 1951 the company benefited immeasurably not only from his extensive musical knowledge, but from his advice on many artistic matters, for he was a man of wide interests and impeccable taste.

The company, in its early years, was headed by Dolin and Markova, whose experience enabled de Valois to build up at a remarkably early stage in its existence an impressive array of revivals of the great classical ballets. The services of Nicolas Sergueyev and his notebooks were obtained, and one by one these important ballets were mounted for the company with the choreography which he had recorded when he was at the Maryinsky: first *Coppélia* in 1933, and then no less than three important productions in 1934, each with Markova in the leading role, *Giselle*, *Casse-Noisette*, and *Swan Lake*. Alongside these revivals, new ballets were entering the repertory all the time, and although many of these have not survived, a handful still remain. Ashton's *Les Rendezvous*, a sparkling *divertissement* to music by Auber, is as fresh today as when first performed in 1933, and de Valois' masterly recreation of Hogarth's London in *The Rake's Progress*, with music by Gavin Gordon and brilliant scenery and costumes by Rex Whistler, is generally considered to be the finest ballet she has ever produced.

Markova and Dolin left the company in 1935 to head their own company, the Markova–Dolin Ballet. Fortunately, they had remained long enough with the Vic-Wells Ballet for the company not to be too much weakened by their departure, and their places were efficiently taken by younger dancers such as Pearl Argyle from the Ballet Club, Margot Fonteyn, Robert Helpmann, a young Australian with an unusual dramatic talent, and another recruit from the Ballet Club, Harold Turner.

During the last few years of peace, Fonteyn and Helpmann were establishing themselves as the stars of the company, and many ballets of lasting value were created. De Valois produced *Checkmate*, to music by Arthur Bliss, for the company's first Paris season in 1937, but it was Ashton who enriched the repertory most of all. For him these were particularly fruitful years, with a number of brilliant ballets following one another in quick succession: *Apparitions*, a study in nineteenth-century romanticism to music by Liszt and with décor and costumes by Cecil Beaton, *Nocturne*, *Les Patineurs*, a skating ballet using music by Meyerbeer, and *Horoscope*, which had a score by Constant Lambert. All these contained wonderful roles for Fonteyn, who in 1937 danced *Giselle* for the first time in her career. She was rapidly approaching maturity, and when, in 1939, de Valois realized one of her fondest ambitions – to produce *The Sleeping Princess* – it was Fonteyn, with Helpmann as her partner, who took the part of the Princess Aurora. It was an ambitious production for the Sadler's Wells Theatre, and its choice for the gala performance at Covent Garden during the State Visit of the French President just before the war indicated how rapidly British ballet had grown in the past ten years.

The company was on tour in Holland when the German invasion began in the summer of 1940. They narrowly escaped capture, and had to leave behind most of their scenery, costumes, and music. But they quickly recovered from this setback, and for the rest of the war, becoming known as the Sadler's Wells Ballet, they were an increasingly important part of the country's cultural life. During these hard years, ballet grew more popular than ever in Britain, and night after night throughout its London seasons at the New Theatre – the Sadler's Wells Theatre was badly damaged during the Battle of Britain – the company drew packed houses. After his *Dante Sonata* in 1940, Ashton produced few ballets during the war years, but Robert Helpmann emerged as a choreographer with original ideas and a strong feeling for good theatre. His most successful works were *Hamlet*, for which he used the Tchaikovsky overture, and his ballet about the Glasgow slums, *Miracle in the Gorbals*, for which Arthur Bliss wrote the score. As for the dancers, while the male side of the company was much weakened by the call-up, two young ballerinas came to the fore: Beryl Grey, a prodigy who danced the full-length *Swan Lake* for the first time on her fifteenth birthday, and the lovely, red-haired Moira Shearer.

By the end of the war, the idea that the state should help to support the arts had become accepted in Britain, and when the Royal Opera House, Covent Garden, was reopened with an annual subsidy from the Arts Council, the Sadler's Wells Ballet was invited to become its resident ballet company. It remained a separate entity, however, and soon the organization was extended to include a second company, the Sadler's Wells Theatre Ballet, which appeared at the restored Sadler's Wells Theatre until 1957. The senior company's move to Covent Garden raised its status to that of a state ballet company, and in a remarkably short time it matured to fit its dignified new surroundings.

The Sleeping Beauty was revived, in a new setting by Oliver

Messel, for Covent Garden's reopening in 1946, and later that same year Frederick Ashton showed that his inspiration had been unimpaired by the war when he produced *Symphonic Variations*, one of the most perfect abstract ballets ever given. In it Ashton's choreography, the music of César Franck, and Sophie Fedorovitch's economically designed décor were wonderfully matched. Ashton's ballets continued to form the backbone of the company's repertory. Among the more successful were *Scènes de Ballet*, with music by Stravinsky, produced in 1948, and his version of *Daphnis and Chloe*, first given in 1951. These were both one-act works, but the popularity of the full-length classics and the company's increased prestige led almost inevitably to the return to favour of the full-length ballet. Three out of Ashton's four full-length works have been created at Covent Garden. His first was the Prokofiev *Cinderella* in 1948, then came his version of *Sylvia* in 1952, and thirdly *Ondine*, with music by Henze, in 1958. In 1960 came his brilliant recreation of *La Fille Mal Gardée*, and the following year, as though to show that he was not irrevocably committed to the past, he produced *Perséphone*, in which Svetlana Beriosova not only danced but spoke, in the original French, the verses which André Gide had written for this musical drama by Stravinsky.

As the years went by, the company's repertory became more and more varied. Massine was invited to produce several ballets, including revivals of *La Boutique Fantasque*, *The Three-cornered Hat*, and *Mam'zelle Angot*; Balanchine restaged *Ballet Imperial*; and Roland Petit produced an amusing trifle, *Ballabile*. There were also revivals of some of the Diaghilev classics, including *The Firebird* and *Petrushka*, by Grigoriev and Tchernicheva, and the repertory was further strengthened with Andrée Howard's *La Fête Étrange*.

The real hope for the future lies in the work of the younger choreographers. John Cranko produced many works for the Sadler's Wells Theatre Ballet – among them, the comic masterpiece inspired by Gilbert and Sullivan, *Pineapple Poll* – before he began to work at Covent Garden. There he has staged several successful works, including *The Shadow*, to music by Dohnanyi, in 1953; his full-length ballet, *The Prince of the Pagodas*, for which Benjamin Britten wrote the music, in 1957; and in 1959 his tragedy ballet *Antigone*. Of the same generation are Kenneth MacMillan, whose unusual originality has found expression in a series of ballets to Stravinsky music and *The Invitation*, and Alfred Rodrigues, whose best ballet is *Blood Wedding*.

In Margot Fonteyn, who has grown up with the company since her student days and has been associated with its progress almost from its humble beginnings, the company possesses a ballerina who can count few rivals on the stage today. She has won her international reputation not only by her superb renderings of the classical roles but also through the many roles she has created in the ballets of Frederick Ashton. Indeed, she is the ideal interpreter of his choreography, and has appeared to no finer advantage than in his full-length *Ondine*. Her contribution to British ballet is enormous, and was officially recognized in 1956 when she was created a Dame of the British Empire – the first ballerina to be so honoured when still dancing.

The company has always been strong in ballerinas. After the war, it was joined by a young Russian dancer from the Bolshoi, Violetta Elvin, who retired to marry when at the height of her powers. Moira Shearer, Beryl Grey, and Rowena Jackson also left the company, but though they were regretted, there were others to take their place, such as Nadia Nerina, Svetlana Beriosova, Anya Linden, Annette Page, and Antoinette Sibley, who is a typical product of the Royal Ballet School training. Robert Helpmann left the company in 1950, and was succeeded as leading male dancer by Michael Somes, who was associated with many of Fonteyn's greatest successes. On the latter's retirement in 1961, his mantle passed to David Blair. The company can also boast several excellent character dancers, the most distinguished of whom is Alexander Grant.

The Sadler's Wells Ballet became the Royal Ballet when Queen Elizabeth II granted it a Royal Charter in 1956. It now comprises a large school, divided into a Senior School at Baron's Court and a residential Junior School at White Lodge, Richmond, and the organization has enough dancers on its roster to supply two companies. As a result of its frequent tours, and particularly its triumphant visits to America and Russia, it commands admirers all over the world. Its choreographers are invited to produce important ballets for foreign companies, and the advice of the organization is often sought when there is question of setting up a national ballet elsewhere.

Other companies, too, have helped to build up and maintain the great interest in ballet throughout Britain. During the war and in the years immediately following, the International Ballet, led by Mona Inglesby, indefatigably toured the provinces with a repertory consisting mainly of the classical ballets.

The Ballet Rambert, the direct successor of the Ballet Club of the nineteen-thirties, has also done much excellent work. Throughout the war it valiantly did its share of touring to entertain the troops and the war workers, and it has since continued to be a vital force in British ballet. Three notable dancers – John Gilpin, Paula Hinton, and Belinda Wright – first rose to fame with the Ballet Rambert in the years immediately after the war, and at about the same time Marie Rambert staged a brilliant production of *Giselle*, in which Sally Gilmour was widely acclaimed for her wistful, poetic interpretation of the leading role. In 1961 the Ballet Rambert's feeling for period was evidenced again when the Swedish ballerina Elsa Marianne von Rosen revived Bournonville's *La Sylphide*, in which Lucette Aldous obtained a remarkable success. New ballets were not neglected. Walter Gore staged a number of successful works during the late nineteen-forties, and more recently Marie Rambert's flair for discovering young choreographers has received fresh proof in her encouragement of Norman Morrice.

Britain's youngest ballet company of note today is London's Festival Ballet, which tours widely and gives seasons in

London at the Festival Hall, where it attracts a very large public. It was founded in 1950 with Dolin and Markova as its principal dancers. Markova left the company a few years later, but Dolin remained as its artistic director until 1960. John Gilpin, who joined the company when it was formed, is now its leading star and enjoys a greater popularity than any of its ballerinas. Many distinguished guest artists have appeared with Festival Ballet, including Massine, Danilova, Toumanova, and Chauviré, while Nathalie Krassovska and Toni Lander have at one time or another headed the company since Markova's departure. The most successful new works which the company has presented are Michael Charnley's *Symphony for Fun* and Jack Carter's *Witch Boy*, but Lander's revival of *Études* is another firm favourite and Lichine's full-length version of *The Nutcracker* has become a popular Christmas entertainment.

THE U.S.A.

Although America has no state ballet company, it has welcomed many great dancers from Europe to its shores and in recent times has become an important centre of ballet activity in its own right.

Fanny Elssler's fabulous visit to America in the early eighteen-forties was only the most brilliant of many transatlantic trips by nineteenth-century dancers, but in the main these were isolated occasions. Adeline Genée had many triumphs in the States just before the First World War, and she was very soon followed by Anna Pavlova and by Nijinsky and the Diaghilev Ballet. Pavlova returned after the war to make several exhausting tours with her own company, and Massine and Fokine also worked in America during these years. But it was only when the impresario Sol Hurok brought over Colonel de Basil's Ballet Russe de Monte Carlo in 1933 that a real interest in ballet as an art began to develop in America. From then on, there was no looking back.

While the visits of the de Basil company were becoming almost annual events in the years before the Second World War, the seeds of a truly American ballet were being sown.

The most important manifestation of American ballet today – the New York City Ballet – originated in a meeting between Lincoln Kirstein and Balanchine in 1933 at which Balanchine was invited to direct the School of American Ballet. Kirstein's aim in setting up such a school was very similar to that of de Valois. It was, as he put it, 'to further the tradition of classical theatrical dancing in order to provide adequate material for the growth of a new national art in America'. The school was established on the first day of 1934 in Isadora Duncan's former studio in New York, and out of it there developed a company called the American Ballet, which gave its first performance that same year, was later engaged for a time as the official ballet company for the Metropolitan Opera, and survived intermittently until 1941. Balanchine was its artistic director and principal choreographer, and among the ballets he staged for it were *Serenade*, to Tchaikovsky's Serenade for Strings, in 1934, *Le Baiser de la Fée* to Stravinsky music in 1937, and, in 1941, *Concerto Barocco* to Bach's Double Violin Concerto and *Ballet Imperial* to Tchaikovsky's 2nd Piano Concerto. With the exception of *Le Baiser de la Fée*, all these were purely classical works that interpreted the music in terms of movement without any attempt at introducing a plot.

In the company's later years, it also presented a number of ballets by American choreographers originally produced for Ballet Caravan, a small touring group which had also been formed by Lincoln Kirstein. The scenarios of these ballets were usually written by Kirstein himself, who often took his themes from American life and legend. Eugene Loring's *Billy the Kid*, which was produced in 1938 with music by Aaron Copland, was the most successful of these typically American ballets, and told the story of a notorious American outlaw of the Wild West.

The American Ballet was disbanded in the year that America entered the war, 1941, and five years passed before Kirstein devoted himself to ballet again. The war years that intervened were not a lean period in American ballet, however, for they saw the formation and growth of Ballet Theatre, which was already firmly established when Kirstein and Balanchine founded Ballet Society in 1946. Ballet Society had a wider function than giving performances of ballet, though this was its most important object. It also sponsored lectures, film shows, and publications, and took under its wing the periodical *Dance Index*, which published many valuable and erudite monographs on the dance during the few years of its existence.

Balanchine was the main creative force behind the ballet performances of the Society, for which in 1948 he produced his important ballet, *Orpheus*, to a score by Stravinsky and with remarkable décor and costumes by the Japanese sculptor Noguchi. Other ballets were staged by a group of young American choreographers, including Todd Bolender, William Dollar, and John Taras.

In 1948 Ballet Society was transformed into the New York City Ballet, when it was offered a permanent base at the City Center in New York and an indirect subsidy by the New York City Center of Music and Drama. It remained, however, essentially an independent company under Kirstein's control. Today it is better known in Europe than any other American company, but in America itself its activities are confined to New York and a few of the larger cities. This is because Kirstein is wisely reluctant to allow his dancers to exhaust themselves touring, for the American ballet public is so scattered that in many places only a single performance is feasible from the business point of view. To a manager who once tried to convince him that a tour with one-night stands would be a profitable venture, Kirstein replied: 'But you do not understand me, sir. I am not in ballet to make money.'

The repertory of the New York City Ballet is mainly composed of ballets by Balanchine. Many of these are abstract works which some audiences, especially in Europe, have found monotonous when seen in bulk. *Agon*, which he produced in 1957, was an important if controversial work of this kind, an essay in expressing music in terms of pure classical dance. Balanchine's creative output, however, is far from limited to ballets such as this. Ballets of many varied types have come pouring endlessly from his marvellously fertile imagination. His full-length version of *The Nutcracker* has proved a sure money-spinner since its first performance in 1954, and in 1962 he added to the repertory another full length ballet, *A Midsummer Night's Dream*, which was danced to music by Mendelssohn. But for many the loveliest of all his ballets is his setting of the *Liebeslieder Walzer* of Brahms, first given in 1960, a dreamlike evocation of the romantic mystery of the waltz.

Other choreographers have also added ballets to the New York City Ballet's repertory, chief among them being Jerome Robbins, who was Balanchine's associate artistic adviser. Robbins has been influenced by Antony Tudor and by modern dancers such as Martha Graham, who command a wide following in America, but he has evolved a style which is both personal and essentially American. He, more than the severely classical Balanchine, typifies today's American school of choreography, which makes full use of modern dance where, by extending the range of the classically trained dancer, it can usefully add expression and effect. Robbins's most successful ballets for the company have included *Age of Anxiety*, which deals with the psychological problems of modern man, and the carefree and exhilarating *Pied Piper*. Another ballet of his, which caused a great stir when it was produced in 1951, was *The Cage*, to music by Stravinsky, a stark and morbid work about the life of insects. More recently, in 1953, he produced *Afternoon of a Faun*, to Debussy's music, a *pas de deux* by two dancers in practice costume who are caught by the audience, as it were, dancing for their own pleasure before a mirror.

The austerity of much of the New York City Ballet's repertory has caused considerable controversy, but it has undeniably produced a typically American style of dancing. Balanchine's choreography has its roots in the formal classicism of the Petipa period, but he has removed its frills and has instilled into his dancers an iron discipline and a classical purity which is relieved by their natural buoyancy and loose-limbed athleticism. This new school of dancers that has arisen in

America has already produced many fine artists, including Maria Tallchief, Tanaquil LeClercq, who was tragically stricken by poliomyelitis when on the very threshold of greatness, Patricia Wilde, Diana Adams, Allegra Kent, and the most expressive of them all, Melissa Hayden, and among the male dancers, Nicolas Magallanes, Francisco Moncion, Jacques d'Amboise, Edward Villella, Jonathan Watts, and the Negro dancer, Arthur Mitchell.

Many other American dancers have developed with the other important contemporary company, American Ballet Theatre, which has the honour of being the first American company to visit Russia. This company grew out of the Mordkin Ballet which had been formed by Michael Mordkin, Pavlova's former partner, in 1937. Ballet Theatre was launched in 1940, with the financial backing of Lucia Chase, a pupil of Mordkin, as an enterprise on a colossal scale. It had a company of well over a hundred dancers, including Spanish and Negro groups, and no less than eleven choreographers – including Fokine, Nijinska, Bolm, Dolin, Tudor, Andrée Howard, Eugene Loring, and Agnes de Mille – were engaged to produce new ballets. Anton Dolin and Yurek Shabelevski were among its original members, Alicia Markova and Irina Baronova joined the company in 1941, and in 1946 Igor Youskevitch, one of the greatest *danseurs nobles* of our time who had formerly danced for de Basil, was engaged. Very soon other dancers began to emerge who were to become important figures in later years: Alicia Alonso, Nora Kaye, Janet Reed, Jerome Robbins, Michael Kidd, John Kriza.

It was for Ballet Theatre that Fokine produced his last two ballets, and he was working on a third, a comedy ballet to Offenbach music called *Helen of Troy*, when he developed pleurisy and died rather suddenly in 1942. David Lichine completed this ballet, which was to remain a popular item in the Ballet Theatre repertory. Later that same year, Massine joined the company as choreographer. He first produced a ballet called *Aleko*, which was inspired by Pushkin's poem 'The Gipsies' and had music by Tchaikovsky and décor and costumes by the surrealist painter Chagall. A few months later in 1943, Massine returned to his comic style when he produced *Mam'zelle Angot*, a ballet version of the French light opera by Lecocq, in which he himself danced as the barber and Nora Kaye was Mlle Angot. Strangely enough, this first production was not nearly so successful as the revival for the Sadler's Wells Ballet a few years later.

Several of the best ballets produced for Ballet Theatre in its early years were by Antony Tudor, who was to have a strong influence on American choreographers by showing how emotional and psychological problems can provide subjects for ballets. As well as reviving *Lilac Garden* and other ballets, Tudor produced a number of new works for Ballet Theatre, including his brilliant psychological study, *Pillar of Fire*, which was produced in 1942 to music by Schönberg, a ballet about the conflict that goes on in the mind of a girl who is terrified of turning into an old maid.

Meanwhile, the American background was not neglected as a source of subjects, and one of the most successful of Ballet Theatre's creations was *Fancy Free*, which Jerome Robbins produced in 1944 with a score by Leonard Bernstein. This masterly little sketch of three sailors who meet two girls in a New York bar overflowed with humour and vitality. Later Robbins developed the same idea in the musical *On the Town* – an important link in the chain of modern American musicals, from *Oklahoma* to *West Side Story*, in which distinguished choreographers have collaborated in the production, using the dance to help advance the plot instead of being merely incidental.

When Ballet Theatre visited Covent Garden in 1946 it became the first American company to acquire a European reputation. In the years that followed, it was to lose its supremacy to the New York City Ballet, but it continued to present interesting new works with a distinguished roll of dancers. In 1947 Agnes de Mille produced *Fall River Legend*, with music by Morton Gould. Based on the gruesome American legend about Lizzie Borden who killed her parents with a hatchet, this is one of the most harrowing of all tragic ballets and owes much of its impact to the intense performance of Nora Kaye, who followed Alicia Alonso in the role of Lizzie and who has since consolidated her reputation as one of the greatest dramatic ballerinas in contemporary ballet. In more recent years the company has gained added strength from the triumphs of its Chilean ballerina, Lupe Serrano, Royes Fernandez, and the Danish dancer, Erik Bruhn.

There are many other ballet companies in existence in the United States. The Ballet Russe de Monte Carlo, which was originally Blum's company, has now become American in all but name and spends its time touring the States with a popular money-making repertory. The most notable new ballet it has presented during its American phase has been Agnes de Mille's *Rodeo*, produced in 1942, a vigorous work, set in the land of cowboys, which includes a roisterous square dance, but its repertory also includes two creations by Balanchine which date from the years before the foundation of Ballet Society. In 1944 Balanchine produced a Stravinsky ballet, *Danses Concertantes*, and in 1946 he staged a narrative ballet to music from Bellini's operas, *Night Shadow*, which was later added to the repertories of the Cuevas Ballet and the Royal Danish Ballet. For many years the Ballet Russe de Monte Carlo was led by the former Diaghilev ballerina, Alexandra Danilova, and Frederic Franklin.

After retiring as a dancer, Danilova turned to teaching and choreography and in 1959 produced two successful works for the Metropolitan Opera, where ballet has become increasingly important in recent years.

America's latest company is known as Ballets: U.S.A., and was formed by Jerome Robbins in 1958 to take part in the Menotti festival at Spoleto. Its success there was so great that backing was forthcoming not only for a New York season, but for a second visit to Europe the following year, when Robbins was awarded a prize by the Théâtre des Nations in Paris. Ballets: U.S.A. is a company without stars. Its strength rests largely on the unusual degree of coordination between its dancers, which is strikingly displayed in Robbins's ballet without music, *Moves*, which Paris was the first to see in 1959.

A number of professional companies centred outside New York have also contributed to the development of American ballet. In Philadelphia the Catherine Littlefield Ballet was active from 1935 to 1941. San Francisco has been the base of the San Francisco Ballet since 1933, and in Chicago the Chicago Opera Ballet is now directed by Ruth Page, who has done much for ballet in America and has many works to her credit, including *Frankie and Johnny*, a version of the famous American ballad, which was first performed in 1938.

A recent development in American ballet is the growth of regional ballet companies. In cities and towns which rarely receive visits from the major national troupes, companies have been established made up mostly of enthusiastic amateurs but in some cases with aspirations towards eventual professional status.

The dance is thus very much a living force in the American theatre today, even if it has taken root there only in comparatively recent times. Its rapid growth has been facilitated by the contributions of many distinguished teachers, including a number of Diaghilev's dancers who settled in America and have passed on to American dancers the tradition they assimilated in their student days in St Petersburg and Moscow: Bolm, Vilzak, Schollar, Dubrovska, Alexandra Fedorova, Oboukhoff. Another link, but with the school of Blasis, was through Cia Fornaroli, who was for many years the prima ballerina at La Scala, Milan, and succeeded Cecchetti there as head of the ballet school, before emigrating to America.

DENMARK

The Royal Danish Ballet, which in recent years has been acclaimed in both London and New York, is the proud possessor of a national tradition that stretches back, unbroken, to the eighteenth century. Its special value for us today is that a number of ballets by August Bournonville, produced about a hundred years ago, have been wonderfully preserved in Copenhagen and are still given there in their authentic style. The

Bournonville style, as it is called, is in fact the old French style which Bournonville learnt in Paris as a young man from Auguste Vestris, and which has since been taught to successive generations of Danish dancers, little touched by outside influences. Its merits are a certain gentle quality – we must remember that the technical innovations which were introduced from Italy late in the nineteenth century did not reach Copenhagen – and unusual lightness and elevation. Also, it is a style that tends to produce better male dancers than ballerinas, a result that may owe its origin partly to the fact that Bournonville himself was an excellent dancer.

The sense of tradition has always been very strong in Danish ballet, but two men in particular, Hans Beck and Harald Lander, have been most responsible for preserving Bournonville's heritage. Bournonville himself saw Beck make his début in 1879 and expressed the desire to compose something for the young dancer, but the very next day he had a fatal heart attack when returning home from church. When, many years later, during the eighteen-nineties, Beck himself became Leader of the Ballet at Copenhagen, he lovingly revived many of the old Bournonville ballets and also Galeotti's *The Whims of Cupid and the Ballet-master*. Beck was not an outstanding choreographer himself, but his production of *Coppélia*, with its great emphasis on character dancing, is one of the most successful versions of this ballet to be seen today.

Beck retired in 1915 because he felt that he was out of touch with the new developments which the Diaghilev Ballet was introducing. A Danish dancer, Emilie Walbom, tried to adapt a few of Fokine's ballets for the Royal Theatre, but their vital quality somehow eluded her. One of these ballets, *Dream Pictures*, a Danish adaptation of *Le Carnaval* with different music, is still occasionally performed in Copenhagen. In 1925 Fokine himself revived some of his ballets for the company, and Balanchine came to produce several works in 1929, after Diaghilev's death, but it was not until 1932 that Danish ballet really began to revive.

It was then that Harald Lander, who had been a pupil of

Beck, was appointed Royal Ballet-master. This made him the virtual dictator of Danish ballet, and as such he remained until 1951. During these years he laid the foundations of the international reputation which Danish ballet has acquired in recent years. With the aid of Valborg Borchsenius, a former ballerina who had danced with Beck, and with the invaluable advice of Beck himself, who did not die until 1952, Lander refurbished many of the old Bournonville ballets. He also produced a succession of original works, the most famous of which were his Eskimo ballet, *Qarrtsiluni*, first given in 1942, and *Étude*, which had its first performance in 1948. *Étude*, which Lander was later to revive for the Paris Opéra Ballet and London's Festival Ballet, was a brilliant exhibition of ballet technique starting with the simple exercises at the bar and mounting to a climax of spectacular feats of elevation and turns.

During the Lander period, a number of excellent dancers were formed. Margot Lander, a very expressive dancer who retired in 1950, was the first officially appointed prima ballerina of the Royal Danish Ballet. She was followed by Kirsten Ralov, Margretha Schanne, Inge Sand, and the most internationally famous Danish ballerina of modern times, Toni Lander, who left the company with her husband in 1951. Among the finest of contemporary Danish male dancers have been Børge Ralov and Erik Bruhn, while the character dancers have included Niels Bjørn Larsen and the great Gerda Karstens. The Danish ballet has always been very strong in character dancers, and this is no doubt largely due to the experience which the dance pupils gain when they walk on as children in the productions, not only of ballet but of drama and opera too, at the Royal Theatre.

In 1951 the company revolted against the stern discipline to which they had been so long accustomed under Lander, who was forced to leave the Royal Theatre. Since then, the problem of finding a successor to Lander has not been satisfactorily solved, and Danish ballet has been weakened by intrigue. The most important production of these recent years has been by a visiting choreographer, Frederick Ashton, whose full-length production of *Romeo and Juliet*, to Prokofiev's music, with Henning Kronstam and Mona Vangsaa as the lovers, was given in 1955. No Danish choreographer has emerged capable of strengthening and renovating the repertory, but a number of modern classics have been revived: Lichine's *Graduation Ball*, three ballets by Balanchine, *Symphony in C*, *Night Shadow*, and *Concerto Barocco*, Roland Petit's *Carmen*, and MacMillan's *Dances Concertantes*, *The Burrow*, and *Solitaire*.

During the nineteen-fifties a younger generation of dancers established themselves in Copenhagen: Fredbjørn Bjørnsson, a brilliant character dancer, Flemming Flindt, who was to become leading dancer of Festival Ballet and in 1960 *étoile* of the Paris Opéra, Niels Kehlet, and Solveig Ostergaard.

The most significant change that is taking place today in Danish ballet is in the training of the dancers. Before Harald Lander left, the Royal Theatre engaged a Russian teacher, Vera Volkova, one of Vaganova's pupils who had taught for some time in London, and the qualities of the Russian school are now being grafted on to the Bournonville style. It remains to be seen whether this mixture will be successful, although some people have expressed concern that the Bournonville style, with its old-world flavour, will lose its former purity.

In this brief survey of contemporary ballet, we have only been able to glance at the more important centres of activity and we must not therefore assume that the work which is being done elsewhere is unimportant, for that is far from being so. Italy, for example, which has contributed so much in the past, still plays a part, though now a more modest one, in the development of ballet. In recent years it has been the scene of activity of the choreographer Aurel Milloss and has produced a ballerina of international renown, Carla Fracci. Today there is promise for the future at La Scala, Milan, stronghold of the opera, where the ballet school has a strong director and a great teacher in Esmée Bulnes. Sweden, too, has a long tradition of ballet. In Stockholm, a vigorous revival took place under Mary Skeaping, who was ballet-mistress of the Royal Swedish Ballet from 1953 to 1962. Here Birgit Cullberg made her name as a choreographer, and several excellent dancers have emerged: Mariane Orlando, Ca Selling, Bjorn Holmgren. Germany is now making a strong contribution. There is great activity and rivalry between the German companies, which enjoy the benefits of being based in municipal theatres, with good studios, ample subsidies, and high musical standards. Interesting work is being done by Yvonne Georgi in Hanover, John Cranko in Stuttgart, and Erich Walter in Wuppertal. Elsewhere, all over the world – in Hungary, Austria, Finland, Jugoslavia, Australia, Canada, even Turkey, China, and Japan, and other countries besides – ballet is flourishing.

So has the great tradition, which we have traced from its beginnings in Italy during the Renaissance, spread across the world and taken root. Today ballet is universally recognized as an important part of man's cultural heritage, and it is the vocation of countless dancers in many scattered lands to nourish its precious tradition. For this is the dancers' heritage, which they receive from the past and which they in turn must safeguard, enrich, and hand down, with its vitality unimpaired, to generations of dancers to come.

A Chronology

1739   La Barberina comes to Paris from Italy and performs the *entrechat huit*.

1740   Sallé retires.

1751   Camargo retires.

1754   Noverre produces his Chinese ballet.

1755   David Garrick engages Noverre as ballet-master at Drury Lane.

1758   Hilferding becomes ballet-master in St Petersburg.

1760   Noverre publishes his *Letters on Dancing and Ballets*, and is engaged as ballet-master at Stuttgart.

       Death of Weaver.

1761   Angiolini produced *Don Juan* (music by Gluck) in Vienna.

1766   Angiolini succeeds Hilferding as ballet-master in St Petersburg.

1772   Auguste Vestris makes his first appearance at the Paris Opéra at the age of twelve.

1773   Maximilien Gardel discards the mask at the Paris Opéra, and the convention is abolished.

1778   Mozart composes *Les Petits Riens* for a ballet by Noverre at the Paris Opéra.

1786   *The Whims of Cupid and the Ballet-Master* (Galeotti).

1787   Pierre Gardel becomes ballet-master at the Paris Opéra.

1789   *La Fille Mal Gardée* (Dauberval).

1796   *Flote et Zéphire* (Didelot).

1801   Viganò produces *The Creatures of Prometheus* (music by Beethoven) in Vienna.

       Didelot arrives in St Petersburg.

1806   Death of Dauberval.

1808   Duport arrives in Russia.

       Death of Gaétan Vestris.

1810   Death of Noverre.

1812   Imperial Dancing Academy is formed at Milan.

1813   Émilie Bigottini dances in *Nina* at the Paris Opéra.

1820   Blasis' *Treatise of the Art of the Dance* is published.

1821   Death of Viganò.

1827   Marie Taglioni makes her first appearance at the Paris Opéra.

1830   Jules Perrot makes his first appearance at the Paris Opéra.

1832   *La Sylphide* (Taglioni).

1836   Fanny Elssler dances the *Cachucha* in Paris.

       Death of Didelot.

       Bournonville's version of *La Sylphide*.

1837　Blasis becomes director of the Imperial Dancing Academy in Milan.

1839　Augusta Maywood, the first American ballerina to acquire a European reputation, makes her début at the Paris Opéra.

1840　Fanny Elssler starts her fabulous American tour.

1841　*Giselle* (Coralli and Perrot).

1842　*Napoli* (Bournonville).
　　　Death of Auguste Vestris.

1843　*Ondine* (Perrot).

1844　*La Esmeralda* (Perrot).
　　　Clara Webster dies after catching fire on the stage at Drury Lane.

1845　The *Pas de Quatre* (Perrot).

1847　Marius Petipa is engaged at St Petersburg.

1847　Taglioni retires.

1852　Saint-Léon's *Sténochorégraphie*, a system of dance notation, is published.

1854　*A Folk Tale* (Bournonville).

1856　*The Corsair* (Mazilier).

1862　Emma Livry catches fire during a rehearsal at the Paris Opéra, and dies the following year.

1864　*The Little Hump-backed Horse* (Saint-Léon).

1869　Marius Petipa becomes principal ballet-master at St Petersburg.
　　　Don Quixote (Petipa).

1870　*Coppélia* (Saint-Léon).
　　　Deaths of Saint-Léon and Bozzacchi, the first Swanilda.

1876　*Sylvia* (Mérante).

1877　*The Bayadere* (Petipa).
　　　Swan Lake is performed in Moscow and is a failure.

1878　Death of Blasis.

1879　Death of Bournonville.

1881　*Excelsior* (Manzotti).

1884　Deaths of Taglioni and Elssler.

1885　Virginia Zucchi first dances in Russia.

1886　*The Two Pigeons* (Mérante).

1887　Katti Lanner becomes ballet-mistress at the Empire Theatre, London.

1888　*Die Puppenfee* (Hassreiter).

1889　Preobrajenska makes her début in St Petersburg.

1890　*The Sleeping Beauty* (Petipa).

Kshesinska makes her début in St Petersburg.

1891 Stepanov's book on dance notation is published.

1892 Death of Jules Perrot.

The Nutcracker (Ivanov).

1894 Zambelli makes her début at the Paris Opéra.

1895 *Swan Lake* (Petipa and Ivanov).

1897 Adeline Genée makes her début in London.

1899 *The World of Art* founded in St Petersburg.

Diaghilev's short-lived association with the Maryinsky Theatre begins.

1903 Petipa produces his last ballet.

1905 Fokine arranges *The Dying Swan* for Pavlova.

1907 Pavlova's first tour outside Russia.

1908 Genée's first visit to the U.S.A.

1909 Diaghilev's first season of ballet in Paris, with Nijinsky, Pavlova, and Karsavina.

Les Sylphides (Fokine).

1910 *The Firebird, Scheherazade, Le Carnaval* (Fokine).

Death of Marius Petipa.

The Dancing Times is founded in London.

1911 *Petrushka, Le Spectre de la Rose* (Fokine).

1911 The Diaghilev Ballet's first London season.

1912 *L'Après-midi d'un Faune* (Nikjinsy).

Daphnis and Chloe (Fokine).

Marie Rambert joins Diaghilev.

1913 Nijinsky marries and leaves the Diaghilev Ballet.

1914 Massine joins Diaghilev.

Rouché becomes director of the Paris Opéra.

1917 Adeline Genée retires as a dancer.

The Good-humoured Ladies (Massine).

Nijinsky dances for the last time in public.

1919 *La Boutique Fantasque, The Three-cornered Hat* (Massine).

1920 Rolf de Maré forms the Swedish Ballet, which exists until 1925.

The Association of Operatic Dancing is founded in London.

1921 Anton Dolin joins Diaghilev.

Diaghilev revives *The Sleeping Princess*.

1922 The Cecchetti Society is formed in London.

1923 Ninette de Valois and Serge Lifar join Diaghilev.

1924 *Les Biches* (Nijinska).

George Balanchine and Alexandra Danilova join Diaghilev.

Death of Gorsky.

Giselle is revived for Spessivtseva at the Paris Opéra.

1925 Alicia Markova joins Diaghilev.

1926 De Valois founds her school.

Frederick Ashton produced his first ballet.

1927 *The Red Poppy* (Tikhomirov and Lashchiline).

1928 Galina Ulanova makes her début in Leningrad.

Apollon-Musagète (Balanchine).

Death of Cecchetti.

1929 *The Prodigal Son* (Balanchine).

Death of Diaghilev.

Lifar produces his first ballet at the Paris Opéra and becomes ballet-master there.

1930 The Camargo Society is formed.

Ballet Club is formed by Marie Rambert.

1931 Death of Pavlova.

Façade (Ashton).

The Vic-Wells Ballet gives its first performance.

1932 The Ballets Russes de Monte Carlo is founded by Col. de Basil and René Blum.

Cotillon (Balanchine).

Lander becomes Royal Ballet-master in Copenhagen.

Flames of Paris (Vainonen).

1933 *Les Présages, Choreartium* (Massine) – the first of his symphonic ballets.

The de Basil company visits the U.S.A. for the first time.

1934 The School of American Ballet is founded, with Balanchine as Director.

1934 *The Fountain of Bakhshisarai* (Zakharov).

Serenade (Balanchine).

1935 *The Rake's Progress* (de Valois).

Icare (Lifar).

Dolin and Markova leave the Vic-Wells Ballet.

1936 *Le Jardin aux Lilas* (Tudor).

Blum forms his own Ballet Russe de Monte Carlo.

Symphonie Fantastique (Massine).

1937 Margot Fonteyn dances in *Giselle* for the first time.

1938 *Billy the Kid* (Loring).

1940 Ballet Theatre is formed.

Romeo and Juliet (Lavrovsky).

Graduation Ball (Lichine).

La Fête Étrange (Howard).

Taras Bulba (Lopukhov).

Dance Notation Bureau is founded in New York.

1941 *Ballet Imperial* (Balanchine).
Le Chevalier et la Damoiselle (Lifar).

1942 Yvette Chauviré is nominated star dancer at the Paris Opéra.
Pillar of Fire (Tudor).
Hamlet (Helpmann).
Deaths of Fokine and René Blum.
Rodeo (de Mille).

1942 *Suite en Blanc* (Lifar).

1944 *Fancy Free* (Robbins).
Miracle in the Gorbals (Helpmann).

1945 *Les Forains* (Petit).
Ballets des Champs-Élysées is formed.
Cinderella (Zakharov).

1946 Sadler's Wells Ballet moves to Covent Garden.
Symphonic Variations (Ashton).
Le Jeune Homme et la Mort (Petit).
Ballet Society is formed.

1947 The Marquis de Cuevas gains control of the Nouveau Ballet
de Monte Carlo.
Palais de Cristal (Balanchine).
Les Mirages (Lifar).

1948 *Étude* (Lander).
Fall River Legend (de Mille).
Orpheus (Balanchine).
Roland Petit forms the Ballets de Paris.
Ballet Society becomes New York City Ballet.
Ashton's first full-length ballet, *Cinderella*.

1949 *Carmen* (Petit).
Nina Vyroubova is engaged at the Paris Opéra.
Sadler's Wells Ballet's first American tour.

1950 *Age of Anxiety* (Robbins).

1950 Death of Nijinsky.
Festival Ballet is formed.

1951 Lander leaves the Royal Theatre, Copenhagen, and is en-
gaged as choreographer by the Paris Opéra.
Pineapple Poll (Cranko).
Death of Col. de Basil.
Death of Vaganova.
Vera Volkova joins the Royal Danish Ballet as artistic
adviser.

1952 Death of Hans Beck.

Symphony for Fun (Charnley).

Piège de Lumière (Taras).

1955   *Romeo and Juliet* (Ashton).

Benesh Notation is introduced into Sadler's Wells School on trial.

1956   Fonteyn is awarded D.B.E.

The Stanislavsky and Bolshoi ballet companies from Moscow visit Western Europe.

Sadler's Wells Ballet becomes the Royal Ballet.

1957   *The Prince of the Pagodas* (Cranko).

Othello (Chabukiani).

Agon (Balanchine).

1958   Lifar leaves the Paris Opéra.

Ondine (Ashton).

1959   The Bolshoi Ballet from Moscow visits the U.S.A.

Antigone (Cranko).

1960   *La Fille Mal Gardée* (Ashton).

The Invitation (MacMillan).

Liebeslieder Walzer (Balanchine).

1961   Death of the Marquis de Cuevas.

The Kirov Ballet from Leningrad visits Paris, London and the U.S.A.

The Royal Ballet visits Russia.

Suggestions for Further Reading

This list includes only books in English which should be obtainable. It is not an exhaustive list.

GENERAL HISTORICAL STUDIES

Mark E. Perugini, *A Pageant of the Dance and Ballet*, 1935.
Arnold Haskell, *Ballet Panorama*, 1938.
Lillian Moore, *Artists of the Dance*, 1938.
Deryck Lynham, *Ballet Then and Now*, 1947.
Fernau Hall, *The Anatomy of Ballet*, 1953.
Arnold Haskell, *A Picture History of Ballet*, 1954.
Mary Clarke, *Six Great Dancers*, 1957.

BALLET BEFORE 1830

Cyril Beaumont, *Three French Dancers of the 18th Century*, 1935.
Jean Georges Noverre, *Letters on Dancing and Ballets* (trans. Cyril Beaumont), 1930.
Deryck Lynham, *The Chevalier Noverre*, 1950.

THE ROMANTIC BALLET

Théophile Gautier, *The Romantic Ballet* (trans. Cyril Beaumont), 1932.
Ivor Guest, *The Romantic Ballet in England*, 1954.
Cyril Beaumont and Sacheverell Sitwell, *The Romantic Ballet in Lithographs of the Time*, 1938.
Cyril Beaumont, *The Ballet Called 'Giselle'*, 1944.
André Levinson, *Marie Taglioni* (trans. Cyril Beaumont), 1934.
Serge Lifar, *Carlotta Grisi* (trans. Doris Langley Moore), 1946.
Ivor Guest, *Fanny Cerrito*, 1956.
Ivor Guest, *Victorian Ballet-Girl*, 1957.
Cyril Beaumont, *Three French Dancers of the 19th Century*, 1935.

SUGGESTIONS FOR FURTHER READING

BALLET IN THE WEST BEFORE DIAGHILEV

Ivor Guest, *The Ballet of the Second Empire*, 2 vols., 1953–5.
Lillian Browse, *Degas Dancers*, 1949.
Ivor Guest, *Adeline Genée*, 1958.

THE IMPERIAL RUSSIAN BALLET

Cyril Beaumont, *A History of Ballet in Russia*, 1930.
Serge Lifar, *A History of Russian Ballet from its Origins to the Present Day* (trans. Arnold Haskell), 1954.
Marius Petipa, *Russian Ballet Master: The Memoirs of Marius Petipa* (trans. Helen Whittaker, with notes by Lillian Moore), 1958.
Cyril Beaumont, *The Ballet Called 'Swan Lake'*, 1952.
Nicolas Legat, *Ballet Russe: Memoirs*, 1939.
Alexandre Benois, *Reminiscences of the Russian Ballet*, 1941.
Mathilde Kshessinskaya, *Dancing in St Petersburg*, 1960.

THE DIAGHILEV BALLET

Arnold Haskell, *Diaghileff*, 1935.
Serge Lifar, *Diaghilev*, 1940.
Serge Grigoriev, *The Diaghilev Ballet*, 1953.
Prince Peter Lieven, *The Birth of Ballets-Russes*, 1936.
Cyril Beaumont, *The Diaghilev Ballet in London*, 1940.
Tamara Karsavina, *Theatre Street*, 1930.
Alexandre Benois, *Reminiscences of the Russian Ballet*, 1941.
Cyril Beaumont, *Michel Fokine and his Ballets*, 1935.
Michel Fokine, *Memoirs of a Ballet Master*, 1961.
Romola Nijinsky, *Nijinsky*, 1933.
Françoise Reiss, *Nijinsky*, 1960.
Serge Lifar, *The Three Graces*, 1959.
Lydia Sokolova, *Dancing for Diaghilev*, 1960.

PAVLOVA

Victor Dandré, *Anna Pavlova in Art and Life*, 1932.
Algeranoff, *My Years with Pavlova*, 1957.
A. H. Franks (editor), *Anna Pavlova*, 1956.

SUGGESTIONS FOR FURTHER READING

CONTEMPORARY BALLET

Mary Clarke, *The Sadler's Wells Ballet*, 1955.
Fernau Hall, *Modern English Ballet*, 1950.
Yury Slonimsky, *The Bolshoi Theatre Ballet*, 1956.
Walter Terry, *The Dance in America*, 1956.
Anatole Chujoy, *The New York City Ballet*, 1953.
Svend Kragh-Jacobsen, *The Royal Danish Ballet*, 1955.
The Ballet Annual, 1946 onwards.

BALLET DESIGN

Cyril Beaumont, *Ballet Design: Past and Present*, 1946.
George Amberg, *Art in Modern Ballet*, 1947.
Richard Buckle, *Modern Ballet Design*, 1955.

BALLET MUSIC

Humphrey Searle, *Ballet Music: an introduction*, 1958.
Roger Fiske, *Ballet Music*, 1958.

REFERENCE BOOKS

Cyril Beaumont, *Complete Book of Ballets*, 1937.
Cyril Beaumont, *Supplement to the Complete Book of Ballets*, 1942.
Cyril Beaumont, *Ballets of Today*, 1954.
Cyril Beaumont, *Ballets Past and Present*, 1955.
Anatole Chujoy, *The Dance Encyclopedia*, 1949.
G. B. L. Wilson, *Dictionary of Ballet*, 1957.
F. Gadan-Pamard & R. Maillard, assisted by Ronald Crichton & Mary Clarke, *A Dictionary of Modern Ballet*, 1959.
Paul Magriel, *A Bibliography of Dancing*, 1936.

Index

161

INDEX

*Some other books published
by Penguins are described
on the following
pages*

THE DIAGHILEV BALLET
1909–1929

S. L. Grigoriev

1411

'Serge Leonidovich Grigoriev', wrote a well-known critic in 1940, 'is probably the only man living who knows the history of the [Diaghilev] troupe from its first performance to its last. ... It is extremely unlikely that he will ever write his memoirs. ...'

That prediction, fortunately, proved wrong, and this celebrated ballet company found its natural historian in Grigoriev, who administered the company for the whole twenty years of its existence. Here is the full story of one of the most fabulous adventures in the whole world of art.

A NEW DICTIONARY OF MUSIC

Arthur Jacobs

R 12

A New Dictionary of Music is a basic reference book for all who are interested in music. It covers orchestral, solo, choral, and chamber music; it likewise covers opera and (in its musical aspects) the ballet. There are entries for Composers (with biographies and details of compositions); Musical Works well known by their titles, such as operas and symphonic poems; Orchestras, Performers, and Conductors of importance today; Musical Instruments (not forgetting those of the dance band and brass band); and Technical Terms. English terms and names are used whenever possible, but foreign terms in general use are cross-referenced. Particular importance has been attached to bringing the reader abreast of new musical developments: there are entries for Concrete Music and Electronic Music as well as references to several works which had their first performances in 1958.

What is a fugue? What is the difference between a saxophone and a saxhorn? When did Sir Thomas Beecham become a knight and when a baronet? Who, besides Puccini, wrote an opera *La Bohème*? These and thousands of similar questions are answered in this book.